REALISING THE POTENTIAL
OF DRIVERLESS VEHICLES

REALISING THE POTENTIAL OF DRIVERLESS VEHICLES

Recommendations for Law Reform

Michael Cameron

The New Zealand Law Foundation
Wellington, New Zealand

National Library of New Zealand
Cataloguing-in-Publication data

ISBN-13: 9781984112491
ISBN-10: 198411249X

Cover design by Gabrielle Baker. For more work visit www.gabriellebaker.space
Contact Michael Cameron at michael@michaeljamescameron.com

For Liv

Contents

The New Zealand Law Foundation awarded me its International Research Fellowship in 2016 in order to undertake research into options for reforming the law to facilitate the safe and successful deployment of driverless vehicles. This enabled me to take a seven-month sabbatical and undertake a study tour to the United States, Sweden, and Singapore. This report outlines and explains the recommendations for law reform that have been developed as a result of this research.

The findings from this research will inform a study on "Artificial Intelligence and Law in New Zealand" which is also funded by the Foundation under their Information Law and Policy Project and is led by Colin Gavaghan, Ali Knott, and James Maclaurin at the University of Otago. The anticipated completion date for this wider project is January 2020.

Acknowledgments

First and foremost, I am grateful to the New Zealand Law Foundation staff (Dianne Gallagher, Lynda Hagen, and Richman Wee) and my interview panel (Dr. Andrew Butler, Dick Edwards, Lynda Hagen (again), and Sir Bruce Robertson). Many other people helped with this project in many different ways, including giving interviews and sharing their expertise; demonstrating technology; helping to prepare and supporting my initial application; reading, editing, and critiquing my work; setting me up with key contacts; releasing me from and covering for my regular responsibilities; and advising on typography and social media. I wish to thank Sarah Abboud, Emma Foley, and Justin Kintz (Uber); Kevin Biesty, Brent Cain, and Ryan Harding (Arizona Department of Transportation); Beith Atkinson; David Bowden, Nick Brown, Iain McGlinchy, and Lee McKenzie (New Zealand Ministry of Transport); Marcus Burke (National Transport Commission of Australia); the New Zealand Civil Aviation Authority; Amy Cameron; Marie Cameron; Peter Cameron; David Crawford (New Zealand Motor Industry Association); Michael Daymond-King; Louise Delany; the US Department of Transportation and the National Highway Traffic Safety Administration; Dan Doughty; Anders Eugensson (Volvo Cars); Katie Elkin, Vince Arbuckle and the legal team at the New Zealand Department of Corrections; Dave Ferguson (Nuro); Emily Frascaroli and Andrew Pride (Ford Motor Company); Colin Gavaghan, Ali Knott, and James Maclaurin (University of Otago); Mark Gobbi; Peter Griffin; Francois Guichard (United Nations Economic Commission for Europe);

Scott Harvey, Joseph Hlady, and Alexa Lee (Civil Maps); Joanna Hayward (Office of the Privacy Commissioner); Sarah Hunter (Google[x]); Dacia Herbulock; Lynley Hutton (Advisian); Paul Jacobs; Suzanne Kennedy; Dr. Anders Lie (Swedish Transport Administration); Andrew Marshall (New Zealand Ministry of Business, Innovation, and Employment); Paul Miller; Dr. Bevan Martin (Victoria University of Wellington); the legal division of the New Zealand Ministry of Foreign Affairs and Trade; Andra Mobberly; Al Prescott and Eric Williams (Tesla); Doug Parker and Matthew Wansley (Nutonomy); Kari Reiterer; Jim Sayer (Michigan Transportation Research Institute at Michigan University); Steve Shladover (Partners for Advanced Transportation Technology, Berkeley University); Charlotte Stapleton; Bernard Soriano and Brian Soublet (California Department of Motor Vehicles); Jamie Tocher; Professor Stephen Todd (University of Canterbury); the New Zealand Transport Agency; Dave Verma (HMI Technologies); and Stephen Zoepf (Center for Automotive Research at Stanford University).

Responsibility for the factual accuracy of this report and the views expressed within it lies solely with the author.

End of an Era

The passing of the horse will completely change for the better the conditions of city life, and work a salutary revolution.

—*New Zealand Herald*, 26 August 1899[1]

By almost universal consensus, driverless vehicles are coming and represent as big a disruption to the transport sector as the replacement of horses with the automobile over a hundred years ago.

For all that time, we have relied upon our animal brains and reflexes to guide people and cargo to their destinations. Those days, as we are told on a regular basis by engineers, journalists, and politicians alike, are fast drawing to a close. While there is undoubtedly a fair amount of hype surrounding driverless vehicles, even the most sober experts working in the field say that within the next ten years, there are likely to be vehicles that can usefully operate on their own with a high degree of safety on at least some roads.[2] In fact, if the most recent reports are correct, the technology is already here in a limited form. In November 2017, the Google/Alphabet subsidiary Waymo announced that it had developed and was

---

1 "The Passing of the Horse," *New Zealand Herald*, 26 August 1899.
2 Steven E. Shladover, "The Truth about 'Self-Driving' Cars," *Scientific American*, 1 December 2016. Mr. Shladover considers that there will probably be "automated freeway systems for personal passenger vehicles" within ten years.

operating vehicles on public roads that drove themselves without human supervision.[3] And the new Audi A8 sedan is capable, according to its manufacturer, of driving itself on the highway without supervision.[4] The Waymo vehicles are not yet available to the public, but the Audi A8 has been for sale in Europe since September 2017.

Given the pace of change, it seems unlikely that technology will be the main limiting factor in the future deployment of driverless vehicles. Instead, it may well be regulation. The aforementioned Audi A8 may be *capable* of unsupervised driverless operation, but in order to obtain regulatory approval and be sold in Europe, it had to be hobbled. European vehicle certification requirements do not currently allow for the approval of driverless vehicles, so the software that allows the A8 to have this capability was not installed in the vehicles approved for the public.

Every jurisdiction across the world is now at a crossroads. Does it prioritise regulatory reform to allow driverless vehicles onto its roads as they become available? Or would it be better to take a slow and steady approach, even if that delays the introduction of driverless vehicles with all their hoped-for benefits?

These hopes for driverless vehicles are well publicised. Because the computers that guide them will not get drunk or distracted or make nearly as many mistakes, they will finally put an end to the daily slaughter on our roads. Because they will facilitate efficient app-based ride sharing, they will take vehicles off the roads and ease the crippling congestion and planet-killing emissions of our cities. Because they can talk to each other at the speed of light, the seething traffic of our cities can be rationally coordinated, further easing congestion and emissions. Because they can be a shared resource in near constant use and can drive off and park themselves when not in use, they will release the vast tracts of valuable real estate currently monopolised for parking and driving. They will spark economic growth.

---

3 Andrew Hawkins, "Waymo Is First to Put Fully Self-Driving Cars on US Roads without a Safety Driver," *Verge*, 7 November 2017.

4 Darrell Etherington, "Audi's New A8 Will Have Level 3 Autonomy Via 'Traffic Jam pilot,'" *Techcrunch*, 11 July 2017.

They will revolutionise mobility for everyone, particularly the disabled, and car ownership will become a choice rather than the necessity it is for many.

But these benefits are not inevitable. And driverless vehicles will not be universally positive. Just as there were with the automobile, there will be downsides. The anticipated reductions in congestion, emissions, and energy use may be temporary, especially if the ultra-convenience of driverless vehicles results in people taking more trips. Even if transport consumers win, a lot of people who earn their living as drivers will lose their jobs. Urban communities that rely on foot traffic for their liveability and character may have that unique character destroyed, as the people sweep past the cafés and boulevards on their way to another pinpoint delivery to their chosen destination. And driverless vehicles may not necessarily prove to be as safe as hoped, especially at first.

Whether driverless vehicles end up being a net positive or not may depend on what we do now and whether we can avoid making too many wrong turns. The law will play a critical role, for good or ill.

Some will argue it is better to spend the time to perfect the law before allowing driverless vehicles onto the roads.

There may be some truth to that. There may be some advantages in delay. But there are also likely to be costs. If driverless vehicles really are going to be safer, then those jurisdictions that delay their introduction will suffer higher road deaths and injuries for longer. There is also likely to be an economic cost, or at least a lost opportunity, for jurisdictions that delay introduction. While driverless cars are predicted to destroy a lot of jobs, they may also create high-value jobs in engineering, software development, and other fields. Those jobs are likely to go to those jurisdictions that allow driverless vehicles onto their roads first. And as driverless cars are tipped to be the first of many technologies in a new wave of robotic automation replacing lower-skilled jobs, they may continue to create jobs for the "first mover" jurisdictions for many years to come. Meanwhile, the "slow and steady" jurisdictions may find themselves with a permanent structural disadvantage.

Each jurisdiction will have to weigh this up for itself and make its own decision. But whatever decision gets made, it is important that it be a positive, informed decision. No country should fall into the role of a slow and steady late adopter by default, or by mistake. If a country decides that it wants to be a first mover, then it will need to make serious efforts to shape its law to achieve this outcome.

The primary objective of this report is to identify the law reform that may be necessary to maximise the chances of fully realising the benefits of driverless vehicles, while avoiding the pitfalls. It focusses on New Zealand and provides a suggested blueprint for what New Zealand should do. It does not prescribe a root and branch overhaul of the statutory landscape. Such an overhaul is necessary and desirable but only as an eventual step. It will not be possible to do a complete overhaul quickly, and it is not urgent anyway because—for many aspects of New Zealand's current law—there is probably no disadvantage in taking the time to devise the optimal policy and legislative settings with regard to driverless vehicles. But there are other aspects of New Zealand's law where it would be risky to leave things as they are for much longer.

For example, it is likely that some of the first driverless vehicles will have no legal route to be certified for entry on to New Zealand roads (see chapter 5). If this delays the introduction of driverless technology to New Zealand, it may undermine any hope for the New Zealand economy to get a foothold in the new robotic economy.

Once driverless vehicles are certified for entry on to New Zealand roads, it is not clear what kind of legal jeopardy those who deploy them onto the roads might face if mistakes happen (see chapters 6 and 8). This is a disincentive to those who wish to try to use and improve these vehicles in a responsible manner.

At the other extreme, it is possible that driverless vehicles could not only be legal but could also—because of the accidental significance of words chosen by drafters of yesteryear who never contemplated the possibility of driverless vehicles—be immune to many of the legal restrictions (such as speed limits) that apply to other vehicles (see chapter 8). For example, under a literal interpretation of New Zealand's current law, it would be possible for a driverless vehicle to speed past a school at 200 kilometres an hour without there being any technical breach of the laws against speeding.

This report attempts to identify the areas of New Zealand's law where time is of the essence and proposes a limited number of insertions and amendments to make it conducive to the successful introduction of driverless vehicles. If any country is in a good position to do this, it is New Zealand. It is a unitary state with no federal/state complications. It does not have any of the legislative constraints that come with being part of a political union, such as the European Union. It has an efficient law-making process and is ranked eighth in the world for rule of law.[5] And it has no established automotive industries and few problems with special interest lobbyists.

As far as possible, this report recommends specific amendments with suggested provisions and exact wording, rather than making generalised high-level recommendations about law reform. It may seem presumptuous to be so exact and prescriptive, but this is an essential exercise. Regardless of the extent to which the specific amendments suggested in this report may end up being implemented, developing them is useful as a way to flush out as many of the potential issues as possible. Many problems and opportunities are not apparent until an effort is made to draft the actual laws. This is a topic for which the devil really is in the detail.

In order for these recommendations to make any sense, this report first gives a brief summary of the history of driverless vehicles (chapter 2). It then explores the likely first applications of driverless vehicles and how they will develop over time (chapter 3). The remaining chapters examine how the current law would apply to driverless vehicles—as a whole and in the many different forms in which they may arrive. They then assess whether and how the law could do better and—where possible—make detailed prescriptions.

---

5 World Justice Project: Rule of Law Index, 2016.

Summary of Recommendations

Chapter 4 examines the inherent legality of driverless vehicles. It notes that there is no explicit requirement for vehicles to have a driver, but nevertheless concludes that there is a possibility (though probably only a small one) that the courts would consider that New Zealand law contains an implicit requirement for vehicles to have human drivers in control at all times while they are being operated on the road. Even though the risk here is low, it may—if it eventuated—destroy any chance for New Zealand to be among the first movers that allow early entry of driverless vehicles onto public roads.

Chapter 4 therefore recommends an amendment to the Land Transport Act 1998 to clarify that there is no requirement for a vehicle to have a driver *(recommendation 1).*

There is a chance that such an amendment could be contrary to New Zealand's compliance with some international obligations under the Geneva Convention for Road Traffic 1949. In order to address this, chapter 4 also recommends that the Ministry of Foreign Affairs and Trade contact the secretariat for the Geneva Convention for Road Traffic 1949 to negotiate an interpretation, amendment, or reservation to the convention to ensure New Zealand does not fall foul of its international obligations *(recommendation 2).*

Chapter 5 looks at the vehicle certification processes that are currently used in New Zealand to ensure that all vehicles on the road are sufficiently safe for their occupants and other road users.

It concludes that, under the status quo, there is probably a legal route available now for some driverless vehicles to be certified for entry into service on New Zealand roads. Under this status quo, the existing mechanisms that ensure the safety of the traditional physical aspects of vehicles (such as brakes and passenger protection) will continue to provide this same assurance for driverless vehicles.

But these mechanisms will not do anything to ensure that the driverless systems for vehicles will operate with an acceptable level of safety on New Zealand roads under New Zealand conditions.

Some might argue that the status quo is fine because (i) driverless systems are too complex for a government agency to assess their safety and (ii) any attempt to do so will simply delay or prevent the introduction of a new class of vehicles that will, notwithstanding this lack of official scrutiny, be safer than their traditional counterparts. The report nevertheless concludes that it would be beneficial to take some action.

Chapter 5 therefore recommends that the Ministry of Transport and the New Zealand Transport Agency pursue a policy modelled on that of the US Federal Government, by encouraging manufacturers to publish a voluntary safety self-assessment of any driverless vehicle they intend to release in New Zealand (including where they offer software updates that would allow existing vehicles on the roads in New Zealand to become driverless) **(recommendation 3).**

In the event that published assessments do not demonstrate an adequate level of safety for a particular model of driverless vehicle that a manufacturer is offering in New Zealand, regulatory action using existing powers—such as recalls under section 32 of the Fair Trading Act 1986 or refusals to issue a warrant of fitness under the Land Transport Act 1998—should be considered.

Chapter 5 also identifies a potential problem in that some early driverless vehicles that may make it on to US roads through exemptions to the Federal Motor Vehicle Safety Standards will not have a legal route to be certified for entry on to New Zealand roads. This could result in New Zealand missing out on being an early adopter with respect to some driverless vehicles (such as GM's upcoming ride hailing fleet vehicles). It recommends an amendment to Land Transport Rule: Vehicle Standards Compliance 2002, to allow for such vehicles to be certified for entry **(recommendation 4).**

Chapter 6 examines civil liability for property damage. It concludes that, under the status quo, liability for any property damage that results when a driverless vehicle makes a mistake is likely (but not certain) to be allocated by the courts to the manufacturer on the basis of negligence.

There are some disadvantages to this. Firstly, even if a driverless vehicle is substantially safer than a human-driven vehicle, it will—unless it is 100 percent infallible—still make some mistakes. While it is desirable and appropriate for manufacturers to be held liable on the (potentially very rare) occasions that their vehicles are at fault and cause property damage, it is an unreasonable mischaracterisation to brand the manufacturer of a vehicle as negligent just because the vehicle was not completely infallible. And yet this is what the courts must do if they are to hold manufacturers liable in the event that their vehicles are at fault.

Secondly, it would be desirable if there was more certainty as to the situations when manufacturers of driverless vehicles, as opposed to other parties (such as their operators) will be liable. The report concludes that while swift statutory reform to address these disadvantages is not essential, it is desirable. It is essential however that any such reform is carefully designed and communicated to ensure it is not perceived by manufacturers as being hostile to their plans to introduce driverless technology into New Zealand.

Chapter 6 recommends amendments to the Land Transport Act 1998 to create a product liability regime to remove the stigma of negligence and ensure clarity as to the situations where manufacturers may be held liable and where others may be held liable instead **(recommendation 5).**

Chapter 7 examines civil liability for personal injury. It notes that this would be excluded by the Accident Compensation Act 2001, and injured people would be compensated out of the Accident Compensation Corporation's Motor Vehicle Account. It concludes that no changes are needed.

Chapter 8 examines criminal liability (including minor infringements such as illegal parking and speeding). It notes that for some offences (such as speeding and failing to give way) there will probably be no liability for any party in the (potentially quite rare) event that they are "committed" by a driverless vehicle. Such actions would therefore be effectively legal when carried out by a driverless vehicle.

While there is an argument that this is a good thing and driverless vehicles should not be subject to all of the same speed limits and other restrictions that are imposed on human-driven vehicles (on the basis that they can operate safely at higher speeds because of their superior ability), it is much too early on in the development of the technology to be arguing that they should be given such dispensations. The public is likely to demand that driverless vehicles play by the same rules as everyone else, and public acceptance of driverless vehicles may be undermined if they are treated more leniently.

Chapter 8 also notes that liability for other offences would be highly variable from offence to offence, depending on the wording of individual offence provisions, and for some offences, it is possible that blameless operators/passengers in driverless vehicles could be held criminally responsible if the vehicle they are travelling in makes a mistake. As well as being unfair, this could also discourage public use and acceptance of driverless technology.

In addition, chapter 8 notes that there are no circumstances under the current law where manufacturers could ever be liable when driverless vehicles "commit" offences. As with civil liability, swift statutory reform is not essential, but there may be significant benefits in addressing some of these disadvantages now.

Chapter 8 recommends specific amendments to the Land Transport Act 1998 to create new categories of offence and ensure that liability for these offences is attributed in a fair manner to the logical candidates (which will include manufacturers in some circumstances and users or fleet managers in others) **(recommendation 6).** Penalties for manufacturers would be limited to fines payable by the company, and there would be no liability for individuals working within the company.

The intended purpose for creating the legal potential for manufacturers to be criminally responsible is not primarily to incentivise manufacturers to develop vehicles that behave in a law-abiding manner. Manufacturers are likely to want to do this anyway in order to foster public acceptance for their products and minimise any demands for further regulation. Instead, the reason is that some sort of liability—even if it ends up being mostly symbolic—is necessary if driverless vehicles are to have the same legal obligations as other vehicles. This is because legal obligations are meaningless if there is no possibility of legal sanctions in the event they are breached.

Chapter 8 also explores the concern that many situations arise on the road where drivers must be pragmatic and commit minor breaches of the road rules (such as driving in the right-hand lane when the left lane is obstructed), and that if the law is going to require driverless vehicles to strictly comply with these rules with no exceptions, then this might prevent them from functioning effectively. It concludes that these concerns are somewhat overblown and often based on an underappreciation of the extent to which the existing law already has the flexibility to allow such pragmatism on the part of drivers and vehicles (for example vehicles are *not* forbidden from driving in the right-hand lane if it is safe to do so and if the left-hand lane is obstructed). It is debatable as to whether there are any situations where this concern is justified (e.g., while some might argue that vehicles sometimes have no choice but to break the speed limit in order to overtake safely, others would dispute this), but if these situations exist, then this is an existing problem with the law being insufficiently flexible. The law would need to be amended for driverless and human-driven vehicles alike.

Finally, Chapter 8 discusses the lack of a corporate manslaughter offence in New Zealand. In the unlikely event that the manufacturer of a driverless car was to seriously misrepresent the capabilities of their vehicles in a way that caused death, this would mean that the manufacturer would not be able to be prosecuted for manslaughter. It suggests that the lack of a corporate manslaughter offence is an issue that is wider than driverless vehicles, and notes that the current government is looking into the merits of introducing such an offence.

Chapter 9 examines the case for the regulation of testing of driverless vehicles. It notes that New Zealand has no regulation at present but that the New Zealand Transport Agency does have a policy to encourage companies who intend to test driverless vehicles in New Zealand, to voluntarily submit a safety management plan for approval. It concludes that the current situation is desirable and there is little to be gained by regulating testing in New Zealand. The essential point is that operating a vehicle on a public road in New Zealand for the purposes of a test is not treated any differently by the law than driving a vehicle for any other purpose. If a vehicle is not competent to drive without a supervising driver, then it should not do so, regardless of whether it is for a test or not. Chapter 9 notes that chapter 5 has outlined how existing laws can be utilised to prevent the use of vehicles (for testing or any other reason) without a driver when this is unsafe.

Chapter 10 looks at the cybersecurity threats that apply to driverless vehicles. It concludes that cybersecurity should be addressed by manufacturers as part of the voluntary safety self-assessment as described in chapter 5, and if it is not adequately addressed, then regulatory action as described in chapter 5 should be considered.

Chapter 11 examines the case for mandated vehicle connectivity and radio spectrum use for driverless vehicles. It concludes that there is no advantage for New Zealand to take action on this in the short or medium term.

Chapter 12 looks at urban planning and the potential for driverless vehicles to transform our cities for good or ill. It concludes that there is a useful statutory framework for local government to influence how driverless vehicles affect cities. It notes however that one potentially important tool (the ability to create congestion charging schemes) is missing.

Chapter 13 examines whether any legislative changes would be required to allow for the creation of roads or lanes that are reserved for the use of driverless vehicles. It concludes that road-controlling authorities already have powers to make bylaws for this purpose.

Chapter 14 examines the privacy implications of driverless vehicles. It concludes that there are significant issues but that the existing Privacy Act 1993 provides a sufficient legal framework for now.

Chapter 15 examines whether legal changes would be desirable to address the different parking needs that driverless vehicles will have. It notes that the New Zealand Building Code contains requirements for parking spaces that would create needless inefficiencies for anyone trying to provide parking catering for driverless vehicles and recommends that these requirements are removed or modified **(recommendation 7)**. It also recommends that territorial authorities re-evaluate requirements for developers to provide parking in the vicinity of developments **(recommendation 8)**.

Chapter 16 examines the issue of whether the law should legally prescribe how ethical decision-making should be programmed into driverless vehicles. It concludes that this would achieve very little and might discourage manufacturers from introducing driverless technology into New Zealand.

2

A Brief History of Driverless Vehicles

In spite of the great increase in the number of automo-
biles, there was a constantly decreasing number of deaths
and accidents. The new automatic automobile, the living
machine, was far more careful in its driving than the aver-
age moronic human chauffeur.

—"THE LIVING MACHINE," *WONDER STORIES*, MAY 1935[6]

Since almost the very beginning of the automobile age, people have been dreaming and scheming about ways to automate the driving process. But terra firma is a dangerous and crowded place with many opportunities for collisions. Perhaps it is not surprising then that the first automatic guidance system for a vehicle was achieved in a more elevated realm. In 1912, the Sperry Corporation developed an aeroplane autopilot that used gyroscopes to automatically control the elevators and rudder in order to maintain straight and level flight.[7] A pilot was still needed to take off and land and also to supervise the autopilot in case anything went

---

6 David H. Keller, "The Living Machine," *Wonder Stories*, May 1935.
7 Robert Mahony, Randal W. Beard, and Vijay Kumar, "Modeling and Control of Aerial Robots," *Springer Handbook of Robotics* (Springer International Publishing, 2016), 1307–1334.

wrong. But this autopilot was improved over the years and became an invaluable tool to combat pilot fatigue.

Inventor of the aeroplane autopilot Lawrence Sperry
(left) in 1923 with aviator Charles Dickinson in a field in
Chicago, Illinois. Source: Wikimedia Commons

The next advance came in a similarly uncrowded domain: the sea. Again, it was the Sperry Corporation, which by 1923 had developed an autopilot suitable for controlling steering and acceleration on ships.[8]

---

8 S. Bennett, "Nicholas Minorsky and the Automatic Steering of Ships," *Control Systems Magazine*, November 1984, 10–15.

Sperry Autopilot Type A-3A. Source: Smithsonian
National Air and Space Museum.

By the mid-1920s, it looked like automobiles might finally be getting in on the action with the demonstration of the "Phantom Auto" in a number of US cities. This involved a Chevrolet Sedan cruising through the streets "without a driver or occupant, with no one touching it and with no wires or strings attached."[9] The trick was that it was radio controlled by a person in a car behind it, so it was really just a gimmick with no immediate practical application.

By 1939, General Motors was wowing audiences at the New York World Fair with its Futurama exhibit. Visitors sat in moving chairs hanging above

---

9 "'Phantom Auto' to Be Operated Here," *Free Lance Star*, 17 June 1932.

an extensive scale model that envisaged a futuristic America in the year 1960.[10] Beating out exhibits from Mussolini, Stalin, and Tojo to become the fair's number one attraction, it featured brightly lit cities with "atomic-powered" skyscrapers, sprawling green suburbs, and rural landscapes of grain and fruit trees. And they were all connected by automated highways along which the public could speed in cars guided to their destinations by radio control. Unfortunately, the "I have seen the future" badges handed to the crowds as they departed proved to be less than accurate. The technical details had not been worked out, and 1960 came and went without automatic highways.

Entrance to the Futurama exhibit by GM at the 1939
World Fair in New York. Source: Rich701Flickr

But hope springs eternal. By 1964, GM had something more concrete. It began promoting the "Firebird," a concept car that "anticipates the day when the family will drive to the superhighway, turn over the car's controls to an automatic, programmed guidance system and travel in comfort

---

10 Arthur Herman, *Freedom's Forge: How American Business Produced Victory in World War II* (New York: Random House), 58–65. 2013.

A street intersection in the city of the future in the Futurama exhibit by GM at the 1939 World Fair in New York. Source: Wikimedia Commons

and absolute safety at more than twice the speed possible on today's expressways."[11] The technology relied upon live electric cables buried under the road, which the vehicle would follow using "feedback control"

---

11 Robert A. Ferlis, "The Dream of an Automated Highway," *Public Roads* 21 no. 1 (Jul/Aug 2007).

of the steering and a pair of "pick-up coils" in the vehicle on either side of the cable. It was ingenious and impressive, and it worked. But it came to nothing. The buried cables cost up to $200,000 per mile.[12] It was not remotely economical to convert existing highways. GM's concept never became available to the public, and the early dream of building automated highways faltered, crushed by the astronomical cost of the infrastructure needed to make it happen.

While this was happening, the first embryonic stages of a new approach—one that did not require any external infrastructure—were beginning. In 1965, the now-defunct but then innovative manufacturer American Motors announced a new function called "cruise command," as an option on its Rambler Rogue Typhoon V-8.[13] It might not have seemed like it at the time, but cruise command can—in retrospect—be looked upon as the first step down the road toward truly driverless vehicles. A descendant of the centrifugal governor invented in 1788 by James Watt to control his steam engine, cruise command enabled the driver to set a constant speed that the vehicle would then maintain. It was the first commercial application of the technology that later came to be known as cruise control. While it seemed much less impressive than a car that could steer itself, it had the great advantage of being able to function without the installation of expensive buried cables or any additional road infrastructure. This lack of dependence on new infrastructure was the key that saw it quickly taken up by other manufacturers and the public. It started the trend of more and more advanced driver assistance systems, a trend that is now on the brink of producing the first truly driverless vehicles.

The next major advance in this new field of driver assistance systems came in 1971 when Chrysler introduced the first antilock braking system for its Imperial luxury brand. Chrysler called its system Sure Brake, and it was designed to replicate and improve upon the braking techniques used

---

12 Robert E. Fenton and Karl, W. Olson, "The Electronic Highway," *IEEE Spectrum* 6 no. 7 (July 1969).

13 John Gunnell, *Standard Catalog of American Muscle Cars 1960–1972* (Krause Publications, 2006), 10. Iola, WI.

Over the years, Chrysler Engineering
has built an enviable reputation for excellence
and thoughtfulness . . .

IMPERIAL LE BARON

The 1971 Imperial by Chrysler
is one of the most luxurious cars in the world.

Yet its standard 440 cu. in. V8 is designed to use nothing more than regular grade gasoline.

Engineering thoughtfulness is an Imperial tradition. The truly elegant interior is made even more enjoyable by the uncanny silence of Imperial's Torsion-Quiet ride. The 127" wheelbase provides generous accommodations for all, yet Imperial, with its standard power disc brakes, power steering and automatic transmission, is a joy to drive. And should you choose air conditioning, Imperial's system is available with the extra convenience of year-round automatic temperature control.

Certainly Imperial by Chrysler has earned its position in the exclusive circle of luxury automobiles. Your Chrysler dealer will be pleased to arrange a demonstration.

IMPERIAL
NEW YORKER
300
NEWPORT

CANADA'S BEST-SELLING LUXURY CAR... **CHRYSLER**

CHRYSLER NEWPORT

CHRYSLER 300

The 1971 Imperial by Chrysler was the first vehicle
to incorporate ABS. Source: Alden Jewell

by skilled drivers, whereby brake pressure is released in rapid increments to prevent locking and skidding, retain control, and reduce stopping distance. It was the first example of the system we now know as ABS. As described by *Popular Science*[14] at the time, "The system has three main parts: an electronic control box, a speed sensor in each wheel, and brake pressure modulators. When a driver hits the brakes hard enough to lock the car wheels, these parts act to keep the wheels turning with optimum braking pressure. And when the wheels keep turning, the car stays under control."

The system included a computer, which was a significant advance over the much simpler feedback mechanism utilised by the first cruise control systems.

Progress for driver assistance systems then stalled somewhat. After the oil shocks of the 1970s, car companies shifted their innovation efforts toward safety standards, fuel efficiency, and reduction of emissions. There was not much in the way of radical innovation for driver assistance systems over the next few decades; just incremental improvements to cruise control and ABS.

Then in 1991, the US Federal Government stepped in. Congress was concerned about worsening traffic jams and air quality. Following initial work in the late 1980s by the California Department of Transportation and the University of California, Congress became convinced that the latest improvements in information technology had created the opportunity to address these concerns by reviving the dream of autonomous highways. It passed the Intermodal Surface Transportation Efficiency Act, which specified a goal of having the first fully automated roadway in operation by the end of 1997.[15] It allocated over $650 million to develop the necessary technology.[16] A consortium of companies, government agencies, and aca-

---

14 Jim Dunne, "4-Wheel Antilock Brakes Give You Sure Stops on Glare Ice," *Popular Science* (November 1970).

15 Intermodal Surface Transportation Efficiency Act of 1991.

16 *National Automated Highway Research Program: A Review*, Transportation Research Board Special Report 253 (Washington, DC: National Academy Press, 1998), 3.

demics known as the National Automated Highway System Consortium was assembled. It included Honeywell, General Motors, Ford, University of California Berkeley, Delco Electronics, Carnegie Mellon University, Houston Metro, the California Department of Transportation, the Federal Highway Administration, Lockheed Martin, Honda, Ohio State University, 3M, and Toyota. The consortium improved upon existing technologies and developed a range of new ones. This included the more traditional infrastructure-based approaches, which relied upon installing new infrastructure like magnets or radar reflective tape to guide the vehicles.[17] But, crucially, it also included other free-agent approaches that did not rely on new infrastructure. There was a vision system called RALPH, which used a video camera to identify lanes and steer the vehicle to keep within those lanes. There were short-range radar sensors that scanned the sides of vehicles looking for adjacent vehicles and other objects. There were rear-facing sensors that used lidar (similar to radar but using lasers). The consortium also utilised radio to facilitate vehicle-to-vehicle and vehicle-to-infrastructure communication to coordinate vehicles with each other.

All of this work culminated in a grand demonstration in August 1997 called the Automated Highway Free Agent demonstration. Advance publicity for the demonstration talked about how "highways of the future may feature relaxed drivers talking on the phone, faxing documents, or reading a novel while an automated highway system controls the vehicle's steering, braking, and throttling and allows for "hands-off, feet-off" driving."[18] The demonstration used a twelve-kilometre stretch of highway located sixteen kilometres north of San Diego. Over the course of the four-day event, 1,350 passengers rode in demonstration vehicles, and they became "the first people to experience such a diversity of automated highway

---

17 C. Thorpe, T. Jochem, et al., "The 1997 Automated Highway Free Agent Demonstration," *Proceedings of Conference on Intelligent Transportation Systems*, 12 November 1997, 496–501.

18 "Demo '97: Proving AHS Works," *Public Roads*, Federal Highway Administration Research and Technology, 61 no 1 (July/August 1997).

technologies in a real-time, real-world setting."[19] There was widespread media coverage, and the journalists were suitably impressed. Highlights included the demonstration of "platooning" in which a fleet of eight Buick LeSabres travelled as a tight coordinated group. The vehicles were guided by magnets in the road. They could "talk " to each other, compare information fifty times each second, and use this information to accelerate, decelerate, avoid obstacles, and stop in unison. The platoon could open a gap to admit other vehicles and then continue as a single larger group.

In retrospect, the event can be viewed as a qualified success. It showed up the impracticalities of some of the new techniques. The use of buried magnets was praised by one journalist, who wrote, "It is very cost-effective to spend about $10,000 per lane mile to buy and install the magnets compared to spending from $1 million to $100 million per mile to build new lanes."[20] This still proved far too expensive to catch on. And the coordination of vehicles was impressive but was revealed to be of limited use unless and until all the vehicles on the road were using it. But the event, along with other initiatives around the world (such as the Prometheus programme from Daimler-Benz,[21] which included robot vehicles called VaMP and VITA 2 driving more than 1,000 kilometres on a public highway in Paris at speeds of up to 130 kilometres per hour) can claim a lot of the credit for the emergence of new driver-assistance modes that were about to become available to consumers in the following years.

These modes included the following:

- The first commercially available lane-keeping system by Nissan for its Cima models in 2001.[22] It used a camera that recognized the

---

19 Bob Bryant, "Actual Hands-Off Steering: and Other Wonders of the Modern World," *Public Roads*, Federal Highway Administration Research and Technology, 61 no 3 (Nov/Dec 1997).

20 Ibid.

21 Alexander Schaub, *Robot Perception from Optical Sensors for Reactive Behaviours in Autonomous Robotic Vehicles* (Springer Vieweg, 2017), 18.

22 Patrick Planing, *Innovation Acceptance: The Case of Advanced Driver Assistance Systems* (Springer Gabler, 2013), 13.

lane in front. If it detected that the vehicle was starting to leave the lane, it issued a warning and applied gentle corrective pressure to the steering.

- The first self-parking feature by Toyota Prius hybrids in 2003.[23] It was called Intelligent Parking Assist and could be used for reverse parallel parking. It utilised front and rear cameras and sonar sensors, together with a computer that estimated the size of the parking space, to guide the vehicle in.
- The first driver monitoring system by Toyota in 2006.[24] It used a camera to observe the driver's face and sounded an alarm if signs of drowsiness or distraction were detected.[25] Volvo introduced a similar system the following year, which monitored the vehicle's movements for signs of drowsy driving.
- The first blind-spot warning system by Volvo in 2007.[26] This system, which won the safety and technology award from the British *Autocar* magazine, used cameras and electronic image processing to recognize moving objects and produce a visible alert when a vehicle entered the vehicle's blind spot.

The US government provided another boost for the development of driverless vehicles in 2001 with a congressional mandate setting a goal for one-third of operational ground combat vehicles to be unmanned by 2015.[27] This goal was facilitated by funding the Defense Advanced Research Projects Agency (DARPA) to run competitions to develop robotic

---

23 Steve Hatch, *Computerized Engine Controls* (Cengage Learning, 2017), 343.
24 Antonio López et al., *Computer Vision in Vehicle Technology* (Wiley, 2017), 117.
25 Ibid.
26 Branislav Kisačanin and M. Gelautz, *Advances in Embedded Computer Vision* (Springer 2014), 51.
27 National Defense Authorization Act for Fiscal Year 2001 (S. 2549, Sec. 217), which stated, "It shall be a goal of the Armed Forces to achieve the fielding of unmanned, remotely controlled technology such that by 2015, one-third of the operational ground combat vehicles of the Armed Forces are unmanned."

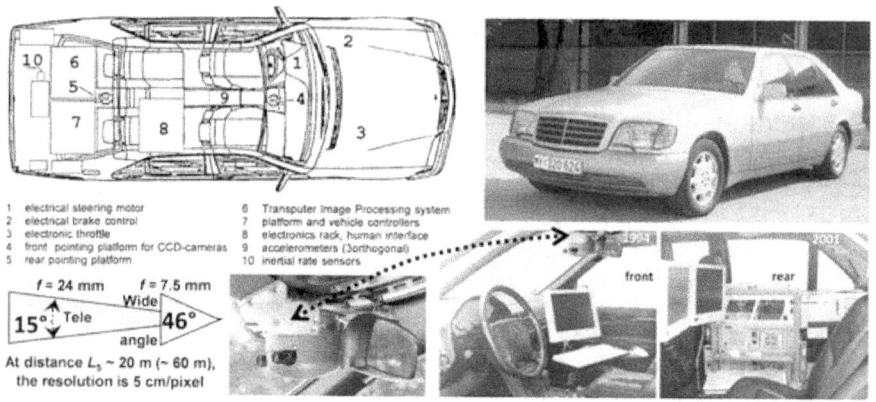

The experimental driverless car VaMP in 1994. Source: Wikimedia Commons.

ground vehicles, with substantial prize money going to the winner.[28] This gave rise to the now famous DARPA Grand Challenges of 2004, 2005, and 2007.

The first challenge in 2004 was a race to finish a 240-kilometre section of highway through the Mojave Desert.[29] Fifteen teams mostly made up of university/industry collaborations competed for a prize of $1 million. They fielded different vehicles using cameras, GPS sensors, and image processing and other software. The vehicles were required to drive themselves without any human assistance, and the route was not revealed to the teams until shortly before the race. Not a single vehicle finished the race, and even the best performer—a team from Carnegie Mellon University using a converted Humvee called Sandstorm—made it only twelve kilometres before getting stuck on a rock.

The prize was increased to $2 million for the second challenge in 2005.[30] This time, twenty-three teams lined up to race on a 212-kilometre unsealed course through rocky and sometimes mountainous terrain

---

28 National Defense Authorization Act for Fiscal Year 2003 (H.R. 4546, Sec. 2374b).

29 Joseph Hooper, "From Darpa Grand Challenge 2004: DARPA's Debacle in the Desert," *Popular Science* (June 2004).

30 Sebastian Thrun, "A Personal Account of the Development of Stanley, the Robot that Won the DARPA Grand Challenge," *AI Magazine* 27 no. 4 (2006): 69–82.

Sandstorm (the entry from Carnegie Mellon University) was the best performer in the 2004 DARPA Grand Challenge. Source: Wikimedia Commons.

near the California-Nevada state line. Five teams completed the course, and the team from Stanford—headed by the soon-to-be-famous Sebastian Thrun—won in just under seven hours at an average speed of 30 kilometres-per-hour. Their victorious robot vehicle was a converted VW Touareg named "Stanley," and they used a different technique to all the other teams. The other teams relied heavily on what is known as "rule-based" artificial intelligence, where you try to program the vehicles with detailed instructions about what to do when faced with all the myriad different scenarios they might encounter. Stanley used a technique called "data-driven" artificial intelligence, which is now more commonly known as "machine learning." This involved the vehicle practicing driving and being trained in the environments that it was likely to experience in the race. It collected mountains of data and gradually learned what worked best.

Stanley: Stanford University's winning vehicle from the 2005
DARPA Grand Challenge. Source: Wikimedia Commons.

Following the success of 2005, DARPA decided to make things a bit more difficult for the final challenge in 2007.[31] Held at a former air force base northeast of Los Angeles, it was known as the "Urban Challenge." The 96-kilometre course involved the vehicles having to perform missions within a simulated urban environment containing obstacles and moving vehicles. Only the best eleven of the fifty-three interested teams were allowed to compete because of safety concerns. Despite the much greater difficulty, six teams finished. The winner of the $2 million prize this time was the Carnegie Mellon/General Motors Team, with their modified Chevrolet Tahoe known as "Boss." Stanford claimed the $1 million second prize.

---

31 Christopher Rouff and Mike Hinchly, *Experience from the DARPA Urban Challenge* (Springer, 2012).

Boss: Carnegie Mellon and GM's winning entry for the 2007
DARPA Urban Challenge. Source: Wikimedia Commons.

The momentum toward driverless vehicles was now gathering steam.

In 2009, Google started its driverless vehicle project, led by Sebastian Thrun, the leader of the Stanford team that won the 2005 DARPA Grand Challenge.[32] By May 2017, Google's test vehicles (which by then were being run by spin-off company Waymo) had driven over three million kilometres and collected mountains of valuable data.[33]

In 2013, Mercedes-Benz released its S-Class vehicles with the hardware and software to provide a range of semiautonomous functions it called "Intelligent Drive."[34] This included steering-assist technology to

---

32 John Markoff, "Google Cars Drive Themselves, in Traffic," *New York Times*, 9 October 2010.

33 Alan Onhsman, "Even for Waymo's Self-Driving Vehicles, It's Intel Inside," *Forbes*, 18 September 2017.

34 Paul Stenquist, "On the Road to Autonomous, a Pause at Extrasensory," *New York Times*, 25 October 2013, http://www.nytimes.com/2013/10/27/automobiles/on-the-road-to-autonomous-a-pause-at-extrasensory.html?pagewanted=all.

A Google Self-Driving Car. Source: Wikimedia Commons.

guide the car through bends and curves. It could predict when the vehicle was in danger of colliding with the vehicle ahead, warn the driver, and stop the car to avoid a collision.

The French company Induct Technology began selling the Navia, a self-driving shuttle in 2014.[35] It was able to drive without human supervision and did not even have driver controls (other than joystick). Its speed was, however, limited to only 20 kilometres per hour, and it was not intended for use on public roads (just airports, university campuses, and the like).

Tesla released its "autopilot" mode for its Model S vehicles in 2014. This allowed the car to drive itself on a highway, staying in its lane, keeping pace with traffic, and changing lanes on demand.[36] The vehicles still

---

35 Michelle Maisto, "Induct Now Selling Navia, First Self-Driving Commercial Vehicle," *E-Week*, 6 January 2014.
36 Alex Davies, "The Model D Is Tesla's Most Powerful Car Ever, Plus Autopilot," *Wired*, 10 October 2014.

needed to be supervised at all times by a driver ready to take over if the car missed something. The vehicle used sensors in the steering to detect whether the driver's hands were on the wheel and issued audible warnings if they were removed. In 2016, Tesla announced that all of its vehicles now came with the necessary hardware to allow for full autonomy without the need for any human supervision but that the software for this capability still needed to be developed (and once developed, it could be retro-installed through over-the-air software updates).[37] Tesla had been (and still is) harvesting data collected from the vehicles of its customers (with their consent) to improve the self-driving software for the vehicles. This is potentially a huge advantage for Tesla. It is training its vehicles much like Thrun's Stanford team trained Stanley to win the 2005 DARPA Grand Challenge but at a much greater scale (thanks to data from the thousands of customer vehicles it is able to leverage).

Then tragedy struck. In May 2016, a Tesla Model S that was operating in autopilot mode collided with a tractor trailer crossing an uncontrolled intersection in Florida.[38] It failed to see the white trailer against an overcast sky. The driver was killed, and data obtained from the vehicle showed that it did not brake or provide any warning of the collision to the driver. The driver did not take any evasive action either. To many people, this demonstrated their suspicion that "halfway-house" systems, such as Tesla's autopilot or Mercedes' Intelligent Drive, were a menace. Research had already shown drivers in a highly automated vehicle were less attentive, more prone to distraction, and slower to react if an emergency arose.[39] This seemed to be confirmation that it was asking for trouble to partially delegate driving functions to a vehicle while expecting a human driver to remain attentive for hours, waiting to correct a mistake from the vehicle.

---

37 Megan Guess, "Teslas Will Now Be Sold with Enhanced Hardware Suite for Full Autonomy," *ArsTechnica*, 20 October 2016.
38 Kareem Habib, Investigation PE 16-007, 19 January 2017, National Highway Traffic Safety Administration.
39 M. L. Cummings and J. C. Ryan, "Shared Authority Concerns in Automated Driving Applications," DSpace@MIT, 2014.

The Tesla Model S. Source: Wikimedia Commons.

The National Highway Traffic Safety Administration (NHTSA) launched an investigation into the incident, with a view to possible regulatory action against Tesla. However, following the investigation, NHTSA ruled that there were no safety defects and decided there was no need to recall the vehicles. It was impressed by data showing that the crash rate for Tesla vehicles dropped by 40 percent after the introduction of autopilot technology.[40] This suggested that any concerns about driver inattention were more than made up for by the crash-avoidance capabilities of autopilot. It was also revealed that the driver did not have his hands on the wheel for prolonged periods and that the vehicle had warned him (in vain) to put them back.[41] Following this accident, Tesla modified and updated the software on all new and existing vehicles so that autopilot mode would become unavailable if three warnings were ignored.[42]

---

40 Ibid.

41 David Kravets, "Tesla Model S Warned Driver in Fatal Crash to Put Hands on Steering Wheel," *ArsTechnica*, 21 June 2017.

42 Jonathan Gitlin, "Tesla Is All about Autopilot and Radar in Firmware 8," *ArsTechnica*, 9 December 2016.

In September 2016, the app-based ride-sharing company Uber launched a driverless passenger service for its customers in Pittsburgh.[43] The service (which is still ongoing) was only a trial; the vehicles were not fully autonomous and required a human supervising driver. This was joined by similar trials by Uber in San Francisco[44] and Arizona.[45]

In January 2017, the New Zealand company HMI Technologies made history by launching the first trials of a driverless vehicle in New Zealand.[46] The trial location was at Christchurch Airport and used Navya driverless shuttles. In September 2017, HMI Technologies again made New Zealand history when its subsidiary company Ohmio launched its own self-driving electric shuttle at the Christchurch Art Gallery.[47] Four models of the vehicle, ranging from small shuttles and freight pods to larger vehicles, are planned for production next year. These shuttles are set to be only the second vehicle to be designed and commercially manufactured in New Zealand since the Trekka in 1973.

September 2017 also saw General Motors advertising that its long-anticipated Super Cruise Feature, which was similar to Tesla's autopilot, would be available for Cadillac models before the end of the year.[48] Reviews of Super Cruise have been glowing, although it was subsequently

---

43 Patty Tascarella, "Uber Debuts Self-Driving Cars for Pittsburgh Customers," *Pittsburgh Business Times*, 14 September 2016.

44 Marco della Cava, "California DMV Tells Uber to Stop Self-Driving Car Tests," *USA Today*, 14 December 2016.

45 Andrew J. Hawkins, "Uber's Self-Driving Cars Are Now Picking Up Passengers in Arizona," *Verge*, 21 February 2017.

46 Michael Hayward, "First New Zealand Autonomous Vehicle Demonstration Kicks Off at Christchurch Airport," *Stuff*, 26 January 2017.

47 Michael Hayward, "Self-Driving Electric Shuttles to Be Made in Christchurch," *Stuff*, 12 September 2017.

48 Michael Wayland, "Cadillac's Super Cruise-Equip Sedan to Start at $71,300," *Automotive News*, 1 September 2017.

reported that its introduction to the public was delayed and wouldn't take place in 2017.[49]

Until very recently, the current state of the art in driver assistance systems were those like Tesla's autopilot and Mercedes' Intelligent Drive that still required constant supervision from a human driver. This appears to be changing.

In July 2017, Audi became the first manufacturer to announce the release of a vehicle that was capable of driving itself without supervision.[50] It has a "traffic jam pilot" mode, which means that as long as the car is in traffic moving no faster that 60 kilometres per hour (i.e., semi-congested traffic) in a physically closed-off carriageway, it does not require the driver to constantly monitor what's happening and be ready to intervene if it looks like the vehicle is about to make a mistake. According to Audi, the driver can stop paying attention and do something else, like watch TV. Once the system "reaches its limits" (which presumably means when the traffic starts to speed up again above 60 kilometres per hour or there ceases to be a physical separation), it calls on the driver to take back control of the task of driving. At the moment, however, European regulations will not allow the Audi A8 to be sold and driven in Europe without having its "traffic jam pilot" mode disabled (more on that in chapter 5).

Then on 8 November 2017, Waymo announced that it had cracked full autonomy and had been test-driving driverless vehicles on public roads without anyone in the driver's seat,[51] and it intended to offer rides within a few months to the public in Phoenix, Arizona.

The latest development (at the time of writing) comes from GM. In January 2018, it announced plans to manufacture a driverless vehicle

---

49 Dave Sullivan, "GM's Super Cruise Is a Marriage of Cutting-Edge Hardware and Software," *Forbes*, 23 October 2017.

50 Aric Jenkins, "Audi's New Self-Driving A8 Is Perfect for Dealing with Traffic Jams," *Fortune*, 11 July 2017.

51 Press release from Waymo on 8 November 2017, at https://medium.com/waymo/with-waymo-in-the-drivers-seat-fully-self-driving-vehicles-can-transform-the-way-we-get-around-75e9622e829a.

called the "Cruise AV" in 2019.[52] It would be a version of the battery–powered Chevrolet Bolt, with the important difference that it would not possess a steering wheel, pedals, or other driver controls. Most significant of all is GM's intention to use the vehicles to begin operating its own commercial ride-hailing service in a US city by 2019.

---

52 Neal Boudette, "G.M. Says Its Driverless Car Could Be in Fleets by Next Year," *New York Times*, 12 January 2018.

3

The First Applications

As we saw in the last chapter, semiautonomous driver-assistance modes have been available for a while and are getting more and more sophisticated. As they get better, they get closer and closer to becoming systems that can be regarded as truly autonomous.

In any written explanation of autonomous vehicle systems, it is, at this point, customary to refer to the current industry-recognized classification system for autonomous vehicles produced by the Society of Automotive Engineers (otherwise known as SAE International). It defines six levels of automation as follows:

SAE Automated-Vehicle Classifications

Level 0: Automated system has no vehicle control but may issue warnings.

Level 1: Driver must be ready to take control at any time. Automated system may include features such as adaptive cruise control, parking assistance with automated steering, and lane keeping assistance type II in any combination.

Level 2: The driver is obliged to detect objects and events and respond if the automated system fails to respond properly. The automated system executes accelerating, braking, and steering.

The automated system can deactivate immediately upon takeover by the driver.

Level 3: Within known, limited environments (such as freeways), the driver can safely turn their attention away from driving tasks.

Level 4: The automated system can control the vehicle in all but a few environments, such as severe weather. The driver must enable the automated system only when it is safe to do so. When enabled, driver attention is not required.

Level 5: Other than setting the destination and starting the system, no human intervention is required. The automatic system can drive to any location where it is legal to drive.

The best systems available to the public at the time of writing (such as Mercedes' Intelligent Drive, Tesla's autopilot, and GM's forthcoming Super Cruise) sit around level 2 or 3 and were described in the last chapter. It is tempting to look upon the progression toward driverless vehicles as a continuum. The vehicles will just continue to gradually evolve and improve and move along this scale. Just as there is no one moment when a child becomes an adult, so there will be no one moment when you can say a vehicle is "driverless."

This would be a mistake. There is very clear bright line. Somewhere within level 3, we get a vehicle that is capable (or at least represented by its manufacturer as being capable) of driving in at least some circumstances without the need for a supervising driver. This is a paradigm shift. Up until this point, we have essentially just had more and more sophisticated versions of cruise control, and there is always a human in nominal control. Everything changes once a judgement has been made that there are some circumstances where a vehicle is safe enough to drive itself unsupervised and the driver is fully removed from the equation. It is especially important for the law to recognize this.

In fact, from the perspective of the law, I think we can forget about the six SAE classifications and instead divide vehicles into two categories.

The first, which in this report I call "supervised semiautonomous modes of operation," are all those modes that still require some supervision (such as Tesla's autopilot) and which fall on the evolutionary side of the line.

Now we turn to examine the second category, which I call "unsupervised autonomous modes of operation." These are the vehicles (such as the latest Audi A8 or Waymo's driverless vehicles) with modes that cross into revolutionary territory, and these are the first vehicles that can truly be called driverless.

Unsupervised Autonomous Modes of Operation
Highway Driving Modes

One of the top predictions over the last few years for the first unsupervised autonomous mode of operation was a highway driving mode. And as described in the last chapter, the year 2017 saw the vindication of these predictions with the development by Audi of its Traffic Jam Pilot for the latest A8.

Despite the higher speeds and greater potential for disaster if a collision should occur, highways are a much easier problem to solve than many other forms of driving. The absence of phenomena such as pedestrians and intersections means there are fewer unexpected events. The range of possibilities that the AI needs to deal with is so much smaller.

An unsupervised highway driving mode would still require a driver to get the vehicle onto the on-ramp and to take over once it exits the highway. But while it is on the highway, the driver could text, watch a movie, daydream, or sleep to his or her heart's content. It would free up time and—more importantly—eliminate those accidents caused by human error and distraction. It would also allow for traffic to move more smoothly and reduce congestion and emissions, although these benefits would be minimal while the majority of the vehicles contributing to the flow of traffic are still driven by people.

Obviously vehicles that have an unsupervised highway driving mode but no other driverless modes will still need to have steering wheels and other controls. They would look like a regular vehicle in most other respects as well. The most conspicuous difference would possibly be the lidar sensors. These are the rapidly spinning sensors that can be seen sitting on top of some test vehicles. They use lasers as a form of radar to build up a picture of the vehicle's surroundings. But you might not even see lidar sensors. Tesla claims that it can achieve full autonomy without lidar. And the Audi A8, which is the first production vehicle to include lidar sensors, seems to have found a way to incorporate them without making them obvious. You might be able to see lenses for the optical cameras. These are visible on the Tesla Model S (though it is hard to notice them unless you are looking for them). Other sensors are not discernible at all.

It is important to note that vehicles currently on New Zealand roads could potentially acquire an unsupervised highway driving mode through an over-the-air software update. Tesla claims that later versions of its Model S sedan have all the sensors and hardware necessary for fully autonomous modes, such as a highway driving mode. All that is needed now is the right software. Tesla regularly upgrades the operating system for its vehicles through over-the-air updates (in much the same way as a smartphone), and one of these updates could, in the near future, see existing vehicles become capable of unsupervised highway driving and more.

Buses or Shuttles in Special Lanes

Another good early prospect is the use of autonomous buses or shuttles in a dedicated lane. The lane may even be physically closed off from any potential intrusion by other vehicles, pedestrians, animals, or other troublemakers. This would obviously be an even easier proposition for an AI to handle than having to share a highway with other vehicles. But the investment in infrastructure required makes it less likely to materialise. It is most likely to occur where existing infrastructure, such as old railway lines, tramlines, or busways, is available to be co-opted.

The potential for this in New Zealand is limited. The northern busway on the North Shore of Auckland is a possibility, but it does not extend in a closed-off or dedicated fashion for the entire length of the route traversed by the buses. Once a bus heading south into the city gets to the Auckland harbour bridge, it must join in with the regular traffic until it reaches its destination at the Britomart Transport Centre in Central Auckland. So this route would be of little use for driverless buses or shuttles that are designed for dedicated lane operation, unless a significant investment is made to extend the busway across the bridge into the central city.

Driverless buses or shuttles used in these lanes might look like existing buses with a steering wheel and all the other traditional controls, so that they can be used by a driver if desired. Or they could be built without traditional controls but with a rudimentary joystick-style controller or similar. Or they could even have no manual controls at all.

Ride-Sharing Fleets

This is the business model being pursued by Uber, GM, Lyft, and a number of other companies, including Waymo, which (as outlined in the previous chapter) appears to have cracked this already. This is the killer app for such companies (although, for understandable reasons, they are reluctant to use that terminology).

The most likely way this might start would be through a phone app-based ride-sharing company gradually replacing their human drivers with driverless vehicles. The experience for customers would be similar to what they currently experience with a phone-based ride-sharing app. A ride to a specific destination is requested by the customer via the app, which locates a nearby vehicle to be dispatched to the customer's current location or selected pickup point. And customers can request a private vehicle or (for a discount) a vehicle they will share with someone else who has a compatible route. The difference would be that when the vehicle arrives, it would not have a driver. It is possible that driverless vehicles could start by serving within regular ride-sharing fleets operated by companies like Uber and with most of the vehicles in the fleet still driven by humans. Customers could then opt in to the possibility of having a driverless vehicle, and if they did not, then they would only be sent human-driven vehicles. There might be a discount or other incentive (such as a quicker average response time) to encourage users to opt in.

The capabilities that a vehicle would need to possess in order to serve in a ride-sharing fleet are obviously much more demanding than a highway-driving mode. They would need to be able to drive safely on regular streets with intersections, pets, children, and a plethora of other hazards. But the advantage of serving in a ride-sharing fleet like this is that any shortfalls in the technical capabilities of these vehicles can be mitigated through careful fleet management. A user might request a ride that would require a vehicle to travel through streets that the autonomous mode is not capable of handling. For example, they might not be adequately mapped, the road surfaces or the markings may be substandard, there may be a particularly difficult intersection, or they might be narrow, twisty Wellington streets, which typically have parked cars taking up most of the road. Or the user may be requesting a ride at a time of the day when it is too dark or under weather conditions or traffic conditions that are beyond the capabilities of the mode. Whenever that happens, the fleet management software would ensure that it only dispatches a human-driven vehicle. The rest of the time, it would dispatch either a human-driven vehicle or a driverless vehicle, depending on what was available.

It is possible that driverless vehicles operated in a ride-sharing fleet would incorporate the capability for company employees at a distance to take over operation of the vehicle on occasion. This is known as remote teleoperation and would represent a practical application of the gimmicky technology first seen in the 1920s with the Phantom Auto. Remote teleoperation would be unsuitable as a way to compensate for any safety shortcoming of the vehicle. A remote operator wouldn't have the situational awareness or the time to come in and avert a collision at short notice. The vehicle needs to be able to do that on its own. Instead, teleoperation would be used if a vehicle gets into a static situation it cannot find a way out of. For example, there might be a small patch of harmless gravel spilled onto the road, and the vehicle is unsure what it is and whether it is safe to proceed. It issues a call for assistance, and the tele-operator could make a judgement (using information from the vehicle's cameras or maybe by talking to people who are there) that it is safe to proceed and instruct the vehicle to drive over the gravel.

Under a driverless vehicle fleet model of operation, the ownership of the vehicles could be quite variable. They might be owned by the ride-sharing company. They might be owned by individuals who are lending their vehicle to the fleet while they are not using them. The important thing is that the vehicles are completely under the management of the ride-sharing company while they serve in the fleet.

A prototype version of this system is already operating in a number of locations around the world. For example (and as described in the last chapter), Uber riders in Pittsburgh can already expect to be picked up by a driverless Uber from time to time. The important difference is that—at the moment—these vehicles are always crewed with a supervising driver (to take control if necessary) and an onboard engineer.

The capability of driverless vehicles to serve in a ride-sharing fleet like this may be an important economic incentive encouraging the purchase of driverless vehicles. Tesla has signalled that it intends its vehicles to have a button (or at least an option that can be selected on the vehicle's touch screen) to join the Tesla ride-sharing fleet. If you are prepared to send your precious new vehicle out to make a living while you are not using it, this would drastically reduce the effective cost of ownership compared to a regular vehicle, which sits unused for much of the time.

There is much concern about the potential for ride-sharing fleets to reduce demand for public transport and make it uneconomic for public authorities to continue providing it in some areas. This is a valid concern, but it should also be remembered that ride-sharing fleets could also be a boon for public transport under some conditions. After all, a bus fleet is just another kind of ride-sharing fleet. There is nothing to stop bus companies from incorporating app-based ride sharing technology and driverless vehicles into their services. They could still have bus stops as before, but the riders would be able to indicate when they want to be picked up and where they want to go. Instead of always sending a huge bus at infrequent intervals, the company could provide a better service at a lower cost by deploying appropriately sized vehicles (including smaller vehicles, such as shuttles, when there aren't enough passengers to fill a bus) at the appropriate times, based on the demand that has been signalled by their customers. The distinction between bus services and taxi services would begin to blur (although taxis would probably be a bit larger on average in order to serve multiple riders on similar routes).

Driverless vehicles used in a ride-sharing fleet might have traditional steering wheels or controls, or they might not. As discussed in the last chapter, GM has recently announced its intention to build vehicles without steering wheels for use in ride-sharing fleets by 2019.

Unmanned Delivery Pods

The size and construction of delivery vehicles today is dictated by the fact that they always contain a human driver who must be shifted along with the cargo and protected in the event of any collisions. Once you take the human out of the equation, you can use a much smaller and less heavily armoured vehicle.

The considerations here are similar to a driverless ride-sharing fleet. Any deficiencies in the capabilities of the vehicles could be mitigated through careful management of the fleet by the company or individual who is responsible for it. But the challenges in deploying such a fleet may be a lot less daunting given that you do not have to worry about injuries to the occupants, and where the vehicles used are much smaller and lighter, there is less potential for injuries to others. Given that speed of delivery for some cargo is less important than for people, they are also likely to be travelling more slowly on average (obviously this does not apply to pizzas and other things for which time is mission critical).

In January 2018 the Silicon Valley startup Nuro AI announced the development of a specialised unmanned delivery vehicle, nicknamed R1.[53] It will be testing the R1 on public roads in California in 2018.

Autonomous Trucks

This is really the same application as that served by unmanned delivery pods but with a greater load and over longer distances. Concerns about collisions would be greater because of their greater weight. It is likely that such trucks would initially only use their driverless mode on highways, using an unsupervised highway driving mode as described earlier. This could allow the trucks to travel without the expense of drivers but would require the potentially expensive construction of vehicle depots that can launch trucks straight onto the highway and receive them off it at the other end. Human drivers would still be used to get the trucks over regular roads to travel to and from the depots.

Another possibility is that trucks could travel in platoons with a lead truck driven by a human driver, followed by a number of trucks that are in constant communication with the lead truck and match its steering and velocity. This would save on drivers and enable the trucks to use less fuel as they follow very closely behind and take advantage of the slipstream. The following trucks might have steering wheel or other controls in case they are needed at other times, or these could be absent. Because it always involves a human driver in the lead truck, it is questionable as to whether truck platooning deserves to be included in a list of unsupervised autonomous modes of operation.

General Purpose Autonomous Driving

At some stage, there will be a general-purpose driverless mode available in regular vehicles that are sold or otherwise made available to the public.

---

53 Andrew Hawkins, "Two ex-Google engineers built an entirely different kind of self-driving car", *The Verge*, 30 January 2018.

When I say "general purpose," I mean it is not restricted to a single environment, such as highway driving. It would have similar capabilities to the vehicles used in a ride-sharing fleet. But it would need to be more advanced to compensate for the fact that there is no overarching management system or company making sure the vehicle is not given a task it cannot handle.

And the term *general purpose* may be a bit misleading because it is unlikely they would be able to go everywhere and do everything that a vehicle with a human driver could, at least at first. They may only be able to drive in certain geographical areas that have been mapped and in which the vehicles have been tested and trained. They may only be able to operate in areas with good road surfaces, clear road markings and signs, and reliable cellular and GPS coverage (e.g., no tunnels). Or perhaps certain types of weather, light, or traffic conditions will pose a barrier to their safe operation. The range of conditions under which a vehicle mode is capable of operating is known in the business as its "operational design domain." It will be critical for manufacturers to clearly communicate the operational design domain to their customers and users. In many situations, it may be possible for the manufacturer to ensure that the vehicle cannot operate outside of its operational design domain. For example, it could refuse to travel outside of a certain geographical area within which the manufacturer has indicated it is capable of travelling safely. In other situations, this may not be possible. For example, the manufacturer may consider it prudent to allow the user to override a refusal if the user considers the situation to be an emergency. Or the vehicle might not be capable of operating safely on an icy road and be simultaneously incapable of recognizing an icy road.

The operational design domain refers not just to the areas and types of conditions that the mode can handle but also to the types of tasks that the vehicle might be asked to perform. One of the important tasks for a general purpose autonomous driving mode will be parking. I do not mean the type of automatic parking that vehicles can do now, where you instruct the vehicle to position itself within a specific park to which it is already adjacent. I mean the ability to tell a vehicle, after it has just dropped you off somewhere, to "go and park." At the simplest level, this would mean the vehicle could drive to a specific park that you have previously saved in its memory, perhaps your driveway at home or a reserved spot at your office. A more advanced capability would be to head for the specific park, but you would also be able to nominate a number of backup parks that the vehicle should try next if the preferred one was unavailable.

An even more advanced capability would be to be able to tell the vehicle to locate a vacant park within a certain radius of your current location, though it is hard to see how a manufacturer could offer a mode that was guaranteed to find a park. What if no parks are available? Would it just keep driving around indefinitely? What if it ran out of fuel or power? Perhaps a more realistic mode would be in conjunction with specialised car-parking buildings that serve driverless vehicles. When you instruct the vehicle to go and park nearby, the vehicle would check with nearby parking buildings as to whether a spot was available. If there was, it would reserve it, pay for it, and set out to occupy it. If there was not, your vehicle would regretfully inform you that it cannot fulfil your parking instruction at this moment.

The Inherent Legality of Driverless Vehicles

There is no explicit requirement in New Zealand law for a vehicle to have a driver. This has been publicly recognized by the New Zealand Ministry of Transport[54], and means that the courts are unlikely to give credence to any arguments that driverless vehicles are inherently illegal. Nevertheless, there is at least some potential for the courts to read into many existing transport provisions an intention by Parliament for vehicles to have drivers. It is worth examining this issue to assess the scale of this risk and whether it needs to be addressed.

A. International Law

Although our domestic law is silent on the question of driverless vehicles, international law is not. The Geneva Convention for Road Traffic 1949, which has been ratified by New Zealand, contains the following requirements.

Article 8

1. Every vehicle or combination of vehicles proceeding as a unit shall have a driver.

---

54 http://www.transport.govt.nz/ourwork/technology/specific-transport-technologies/road-vehicle/autonomous-vehicles/

2. Draught, pack or saddle animals shall have a driver, and cattle shall be accompanied, except in special areas which shall be marked at the points of entry.
3. Convoys of vehicles and animals shall have the number of drivers prescribed by domestic regulations.
4. Convoys shall, if necessary, be divided into sections of moderate length, and be sufficiently spaced out for the convenience of traffic. This provision does not apply to regions where migration of nomads occurs.
5. Drivers shall at all times be able to control their vehicles or guide their animals. When approaching other road users, they shall take such precautions as may be required for the safety of the latter.

While it seems very concerned with nomads and pack animals, article 8.1 would also—on its face—appear to be prohibiting the modern phenomenon of driverless vehicles. It is not entirely clear what problem the drafters of this sixty-eight-year-old convention were attempting to address here. Did they witness a demonstration of the Phantom Auto[55] in the 1920s and decide that kind of thing needed to be stamped out? Or does it have something to do with the mention of a "combination of vehicles proceeding as a unit." In other words, if one vehicle was towing a series of vehicles, was it requiring every vehicle in the train to have its own driver? Whatever was intended, there is no question that a literal interpretation rules out the use of driverless vehicles.

B. The Effect of International Law and Its Implementation

Even if the convention is interpreted as prohibiting driverless vehicles, it cannot have any direct legal effect in New Zealand. Despite New Zealand's ratification of the convention, no part of it will be construed by the courts as having any direct legal effect. Its influence is mainly limited

---

55 See chapter 1.

to New Zealand's obligation under international law to incorporate its requirements into our domestic law. It could be argued that our lack of any explicit requirement for vehicles to have drivers means New Zealand has failed to do this and should be receiving adverse reports from the secretariat informing us of our obligation to do so. But New Zealand has received no such reports. And if it were to do so, New Zealand could possibly argue that the objective of having no vehicles without drivers has, until now, been achieved without legislative action, because it is impossible for a vehicle to operate without a driver. But of course that's not true anymore (and perhaps it never was true if you interpret towed vehicles as being among the vehicles that article 8.1 was requiring to have a driver[56]).

C. Interpretation of Domestic Legislation

While it can have no direct effect, the courts will always make an attempt to interpret our domestic legislation in a way that is consistent with our international obligations, if at all possible. And our domestic legislation is littered with provisions that seem to be written with the implicit assumption that all vehicles have drivers.

For example, section 22 of the Land Transport Act 1998 requires the driver or rider of a vehicle that has been involved in an accident to stop and ascertain whether a person has been injured and render all practicable assistance. Parliament's objective here is to ensure that the injured receive help, and it could be argued that this objective is frustrated if unmanned vehicles can collide into other vehicles and injure the occupants without any possibility of those occupants receiving help from the other vehicle. And the courts could therefore be persuaded that Parliament, in enacting section 22, intended that it be consistent with the convention and that it must include an implicit requirement for all vehicles to have drivers (or at least conscious adult occupants).

Another example is the prohibition in clause 5.1 of Land Transport (Road User) Rule 2004 against speeding. This applies to a driver who is

---

56 There is no requirement in New Zealand for a towed vehicle to have a driver.

driving a vehicle,[57] and so arguably, there is no prohibition against a driverless vehicle speeding and no offence or offender when it does. Again, it could be argued that Parliament can never have intended that any vehicle be permitted to speed with impunity. And so it must have intended clause 5.1 to be compliant with the convention by containing an underlying implicit requirement for all vehicles to have a driver.

D. A Necessary Clarification to Domestic Legislation?

If there is a risk of the courts concluding that driverless vehicles are inherently illegal on New Zealand roads, it is unclear how this risk would be manifested. The risk seems slight. Nevertheless, if we wish to ensure that driverless vehicles are legal on our roads (and I think we should), then it would be prudent to include a provision in the Land Transport Act 1998 clarifying this (see recommendation 1 below). This is not to discount the concerns I mentioned previously about driverless vehicles frustrating the purpose of many of our existing transport provisions, but there are—as will be outlined in later chapters—other ways to address this.

E. Harmonisation with International Law

If we are to include an explicit provision authorising the presence of vehicles without a driver, then we probably need to do something about the Geneva Convention for Road Traffic. It is one thing to neglect to include provisions that explicitly give effect to its apparent requirement for all vehicles to have drivers. It is quite another to include an explicit provision that appears to directly contradict this requirement.

The first step in trying to resolve this is for the Ministry of Foreign Affairs and Trade (MFAT) to contact the secretariat for the convention and ask whether such a provision would be regarded as being inconsistent

---

57 Clause 5.1 of Land Transport (Road User) Rule 2004 prohibits speeding, and regulations 3 and 4 and schedule 1 of the Land Transport (Offences and Penalties) Regulations 1999 specify it as a regular offence and an infringement offence.

with the convention. Despite the apparent contradiction, it is possible that the secretariat would find a way of interpreting the convention to allow this.

If it cannot or will not do this, then there are a number of other ways for MFAT to proceed. It could seek to make a reservation against article 8.1. There does not appear to be a reservation provision in the convention, but that does not necessarily mean it cannot be done. Or MFAT could withdraw from the convention altogether, although that would be a drastic step. A longer-term solution would be to amend the convention to remove the apparent requirement in article 8.1. The convention does include an amending procedure, but it requires the contracting parties to agree. While it seems likely that the convention would be amended eventually (unless the issue can be solved first by interpretation), this might take a while.

Recommendations

My view is that we need to ensure that there is no risk at all of the courts concluding that the law contains a blanket prohibition against driverless vehicles. This risk is not high, but it would be prudent to remove it altogether. I make the following recommendations to achieve this.\

Recommendation 1

Amend the Land Transport Act 1998 to include a provision, along the lines set out here, that explicitly allows vehicles to be operated without a driver on New Zealand roads.

9A   No requirement for vehicles to have a driver

For the avoidance of doubt, there is no requirement for a vehicle to have a driver.

Recommendation 2

The Ministry of Foreign Affairs and Trade should contact the secretariat for the Geneva Convention for Road Traffic 1949 seeking an interpretation of article 8.1 that allows New Zealand to include a provision in the Land Transport Act 1998 that explicitly allows vehicles to be operated on our roads without a driver. Failing this, MFAT should seek to make a reservation against article 8.1, amend the convention, or (as a last resort) withdraw from the convention.

5

Ensuring the Safety of Driverless Vehicles

New Zealand already has detailed vehicle certification processes that are designed to ensure that all vehicles on the road are sufficiently safe for their occupants and for all other road users. Vehicles must be inspected before they can be certified for entry into service on to our roads, and they are subject to further periodic inspections to ensure that they remain roadworthy.

These processes will be important in ensuring the safety of the new breed of driverless vehicles. It is important to examine whether they are fit for purpose. Are they up to the job? And are they sufficiently flexible to allow driverless vehicles onto our roads where this is appropriate?

A. New Zealand's Vehicle Certification Process

At some point soon, a vehicle model will become available that is claimed by its manufacturer to be capable of driving itself in at least some circumstances without any supervision by a human driver. As explained in earlier chapters, such a vehicle may already exist in the form of the latest Audi A8. Before such a vehicle can be certified for entry into service on New Zealand roads, it needs to be inspected and certified by a New Zealand vehicle inspector.[58] The inspector will only certify the vehicle if satisfied that the vehicle meets the requirements as set out at clause 6.4(1)

---

58 Clause 6.3(1)(a) of Land Transport Rule: Vehicle Standards Compliance 2002.

of Land Transport Rule: Vehicle Standards Compliance 2002. There are a number of these requirements, including a general requirement that it is "safe to be operated," but the key requirement is that it complies with one of the sets of overseas vehicle standards that are recognized in New Zealand.[59] The standards that are recognized are those from the United States, Europe, Australia, or Japan, plus the UN standards, which are incorporated into some of these national requirements.

It is necessary now to examine the motor vehicle approval systems of these jurisdictions to see how they work, and how they will affect the certification of driverless vehicles for entry on to New Zealand roads.

B. The European Motor Vehicle Approval System

The European system is governed by Directive 2007/46/EC of the European Parliament. This directive requires manufacturers to subject examples of their vehicles for testing by a technical service company, with a view to obtaining type-approval from an official vehicle approval authority (there are many different such authorities in the different member states). The technical service company carries out extensive inspection and testing to evaluate the vehicle against the requirements of the directive. These requirements are mostly derived from references to regulations produced by the United Nations Economic Commission for Europe, more commonly known as the UNECE regulations.

---

59 These standards are described as "applicable requirements" in clause 6.4(1)(c) of Land Transport Rule: Vehicle Standards Compliance 2002. This term has been defined in part 2 of the rule as "any requirement specified or incorporated in an Act, regulation, code or rule listed in Schedule 1 that applies to the design, construction, condition, equipment, modification, repair or maintenance of a specific vehicle." Schedule 1 lists seventeen Land Transport Rules that govern different aspects of a vehicle's construction. Each of these seventeen rules contains references to "approved vehicle standards" that are recognized in relation to the different aspects of vehicles covered by the different rules. These "approved vehicle standards" are all the UN, US, European, Australian, or Japanese standards against which the compliance of all the different aspects of incoming vehicles may be measured and certified.

The reason these UN regulations have been incorporated into European law dates back to a 1958 convention with the rather unwieldy name "Agreement Concerning the Adoption of Uniform Technical Prescriptions for Wheeled Vehicles, Equipment and Parts which Can Be Fitted and/or Be Used on Wheeled Vehicles and the Conditions for Reciprocal Recognition of Approvals Granted on the Basis of These Prescriptions." This convention comes under the ambit of the United Nations World Forum for Harmonization of Vehicle Regulations. The initial objective of the convention was to develop common standards for all of Europe in order to prevent countries using their national regulations as trade barriers to protect local industry, while also promoting a high level of safety and acceptable environmental impact for European vehicles. It has since transcended its European origins, and now most of the world, including New Zealand (but with the notable exceptions of the United States and Canada) has signed up to the 1958 convention. Signatories to the convention agree to recognise approvals granted by other countries as long as those approvals were granted in accordance with the UNECE regulations. There are many different sets of regulations governing different aspects of a vehicle's construction and performance. For example, the steering equipment for vehicles is governed by UNECE 79: Uniform Provisions Concerning the Approval of Vehicles with Regard to Steering Equipment.

An example of the European approval system in action is provided by the approval process for the US-manufactured Tesla Model S. This model was introduced in the United States on 22 June 2012. It was not able to be imported into Europe on that date because it did not have European approval yet. And it was not able to be imported into New Zealand because Tesla had only produced a left-hand drive variant for the US market. Tesla then designed and produced a European version of the model to meet the European / UNECE regulations. This time the model had left-hand and right-hand drive variants (the latter to serve European markets such as the UK and Ireland that drive on the left side). Examples of the vehicles were subjected to rigorous inspection and testing by a technical service company and were given type-approval in 2013 by a Dutch vehicle approval agency known as RDW.[60] This allowed them to be imported into and sold in Europe by early August 2013. This also meant that right-hand drive variants were available to be imported into New Zealand (though the first one was not imported until November 2014).

The initial version of the Model S, as introduced to the United States in 2012, did not have the semiautonomous mode known as autopilot. This did not come until October 2014, when the first Model S vehicles with the hardware and software necessary for autopilot were shipped to US customers. In order to be imported into and sold in Europe, the European version of these autopilot-equipped Model S vehicles could not rely on the existing type-approval from RDW. The new capabilities of the vehicle were not considered to be covered by that type-approval, and so it was necessary to get what is known as an extension to the type approval. Tesla provided examples of the new autopilot-equipped vehicles for inspection and testing. On 25 October 2015, it was reported by RDW[61] that it had approved autopilot for the Model S (and there was a tweet from Tesla's CEO Elon Musk on the same day, saying that autopilot was approved everywhere except Japan). This then allowed these vehicles into Europe, and they could also be imported into New Zealand from this point.

When the first driverless vehicles are developed, they may have difficulty following this same path into New Zealand. There is much uncertainty as to whether it is possible for a truly driverless vehicle to get approval under the current versions of the UNECE regulations. This is primarily because of the way that one of those regulations—UNECE 79, dealing with steering—has been drafted and how it is interpreted. This regulation is commonly regarded as being "problematic for automated cars."[62]

---

60 As reported in Tesla's shareholder report at http://files.shareholder.com/downloads/ABEA-4CW8X0/3015878807x0xS1193125-14-69681/1318605/filing.pdf.

61 Press release from RDW dated 25 October 2015, at https://www.rdw.nl/overrdw/Paginas/Autopilot-bij-update-Tesla-goedgekeurd-voor-Europa--.aspx.

62 L. Lutz, "Automated Vehicles in the EU: Proposals to Amend the Type Approval Framework of Driver Conduct," *Casualty Matters International* (March 2016).

The UNECE itself appears to believe that amendments to UNECE 79 are needed to pave the way for automated driving.[63]

In particular, the UNECE talks about "removing the current limitation of automatic steering functions to driving conditions below 10 km/h." It is not entirely clear—when looking at the wording of UNECE 79—why these changes are essential. The limitation that has been marked for removal would appear to be coming from paragraph 5.1.6.1, which requires that "whenever the Automatically Commanded Steering function becomes operational...the control action shall be automatically disabled if the vehicle speed exceeds the set limit of 10 km/h by more than 20 per cent..." The concern seems to be that this paragraph will rule out driverless vehicles travelling faster than 10 to 12 kilometres per hour, presumably on the basis that all driverless vehicles will need to make use of an "automatically commanded steering function" that must be disabled above these speeds.

But this does not follow from the definition of an "automatically commanded steering function." Paragraph 2.3.4.1 defines this as a "...function...where actuation of the steering system can result from automatic evaluation of signals initiated on-board the vehicle...to generate continuous control action in order to assist the driver in following a particular path, *in low speed manoeuvring or parking situations*" (emphasis added). As can be seen by the words emphasised in italics, this definition—when read literally—is somewhat self-limiting. If a driverless vehicle is using a system to steer itself at high speeds, then that system does not meet the definition, and so it is not required under paragraph 5.1.6.1 to be deactivated above 10 to 12 kilometres per hour. In addition, it is a system that "assists the driver" and so a system that operates without a driver at all would not be captured by the definition.

Adding to this confusion, it is not clear what the basis was for Tesla's autopilot function to have been approved under UNECE 79 by RDW in

---

63 "UNECE Paves the Way for Automated Driving by Updating UN International Convention," UNECE press release, 23 March 2016.

2015. If one is of the opinion that UNECE 79 in its current form poses an obstacle for driverless vehicles, then this must involve departing from the literal meaning of the provisions described above and taking some sort of purposive interpretation that automated steering above 10 to 12 kilometres per hour is not allowed. But if you take that approach, then the provisions should pose an identical obstacle for autopilot. Autopilot, despite not being a fully driverless mode, meets all of other aspects of the definition. It is a system where "the actuation of the steering system can result from automatic evaluation of signals initiated on board the vehicle." And this generates "continuous control action in order to assist the driver in following a particular path."

Surely then, Tesla's autopilot should not have been approved, because it is not disabled at speeds in excess of 10 to 12 kilometres per hour. The documentation surrounding the decision is not publicly available, so we cannot find out the reasoning here. I have posed this question about how it could have been approved to various experts on the European system and—while no one has agreed to go on the record—they have indicated that RDW did not appear to be applying UNECE 79 correctly when it approved autopilot, and there may have been political pressure for it to do what it did.

This raises the possibility that further political pressure could result in fully driverless vehicles being approved under the current provisions, despite the belief by UNECE and others that this is not possible without them being amended first.

It seems more likely, however, that we would need to wait for amendments. When will these amendments arrive? This is also not clear. The latest press release from the UNECE on this topic was in March 2016.[64] It said it expected that work "evaluating the technical requirements that these innovations enabling automated driving shall comply with to ensure safety" would be completed in September 2016 with a view to adoption

---

64 "UNECE Paves the Way for Automated Driving by Updating UN International Convention," UNECE press release, 23 March 2016.

in regulations by 2017. This timeframe has not been met, and there is no further official comment as to when progress might be expected. I have received unofficial comment that a new version of UNECE 79 might be proposed in April 2018, but whether this will eventuate is highly uncertain.

Another way that driverless vehicles could obtain approval in Europe is if an individual member state was to grant an exemption under article 20 of Directive 2007/46/EC. Article 20 allows member states to grant provisional-type approvals in relation to systems that utilise new technologies. These approvals will apply in the state itself, and other states can choose to accept the provisional approval in their territory. The European Commission will then begin a process to either accept or reject the provisional approval. It is quite possible that member states may seek to use this mechanism if they grow frustrated with lack of progress in amending the UNECE regulations. If they did, it is important to recognize that New Zealand does not recognize these provisional approvals. Our Land Transport Rules require compliance with named European Directives or UNECE regulations.[65]

C. The US Motor Vehicle Approval System

The United States has not signed up to the 1958 convention mentioned earlier, and, as a result, its system is very different from the system used in Europe and almost everywhere else (except Canada). Under the US system, there is no need for any kind of official agency (akin to the vehicle approval agencies in Europe) to inspect, test, and approve the new models for compliance with the vehicle standards—known as the Federal Motor Vehicle Safety Standards (FMVSS)—used in the US. The FMVSS do contain very stringent requirements for testing and inspection, but this can be done by the manufacturer itself. The manufacturer is then able to self-certify compliance of a new type of vehicle with the FMVSS and affix

---

65 This is in line with the Transport Regulatory Policy Statement (2012 edition), which outlines the expectation that legislation and processes will be certain and transparent. See page 7 of the statement at http://www.transport.govt.nz/assets/Import/Documents/Transport-Regulatory-Policy-Statement-2012-Edition-Issued-4-May-2012.pdf.

a small plate to each individual vehicle of that model or type in order to signify this compliance.

Concern about conflicts of interest in having the manufacturers testing and certifying their own vehicles is mitigated by the National Highway Traffic Safety Administration (NHTSA) having extensive market surveillance powers and resources to test vehicles after they have been certified and, if necessary, to take regulatory action, such as recalls. NHTSA does not test all models and types of vehicles against all aspects of the FMVSS. It employs a "risk-based selection process to strategically select which standards and vehicles to test."[66] This provides an incentive, similar to that provided by the threat of audit by a tax authority, for the manufacturers to take self-certification seriously.

The other way in which the US system differs substantially from the European system is that—for the moment—the FMVSS do not have any provisions that would represent a serious impediment to the self-certification of fully autonomous vehicles.[67] As long as the vehicle does not significantly diverge from conventional vehicle design, then the additional capability of having a driverless mode does not make it any more difficult for the vehicle to be certified. The effect of this can be seen already in the way it applied to the Tesla's autopilot when it was first released. Because there was nothing in the FMVSS that governed self-steering or other systems utilised by autopilot, it was not necessary[68] for the manufacturer to carry out any tests and self-certify the new vehicles as compliant.

This does not mean it is the Wild West in the United States with respect to driverless systems. As outlined in the Federal Automated Vehicles Policy

---

66 Federal Automated Vehicles Policy, September 2016, 71.

67 See A. Kim et al., *Review of Federal Motor Vehicle Safety Standards (FMVSS) for Automated Vehicles. Preliminary Report—March 2016*, US Department of Transportation, John A. Volpe National Transportation Systems Center. At page vIII, this concludes that "there are few barriers for automated vehicles to comply with the FMVSS, as long as the vehicle does not significantly diverge from conventional vehicle design."

68 At least not legally necessary. Presumably, Tesla would have nevertheless carried out significant safety testing.

released by NHTSA in September 2016,[69] new driverless vehicles will, like traditional vehicles, be subject to NHTSA's post-certification market surveillance and enforcement regimes. This includes powers for NHTSA to "recall vehicles that pose an unreasonable risk to safety even when there is no applicable FMVSS." This last point is important because it means that NHTSA has powers to recall driverless vehicles even though they might have been self-certified and fully comply with the FMVSS standards (which—as noted earlier—they probably will, because there is no standard applying to driverless systems).

There may be questions about how effective these powers will be without standards to back them up and provide a defined level of acceptable risk, but they at least provide a level of assurance. In order to help NHTSA determine whether a particular model of driverless vehicle is safe or not and whether it should be exercising any of these powers to protect public safety, NHTSA's latest automated vehicles policy[70] encourages manufacturers to publish a "Voluntary Safety Self-Assessment" to demonstrate the safety of their vehicles. This self-assessment should cover the following elements:

- system safety
- operational design domain
- object and event detection response
- fallback (minimal risk condition)
- validation methods
- human machine interface
- vehicle cybersecurity
- crashworthiness
- postcrash behaviour
- data recording

---

69 Now superceded by "Automated Driving Systems 2.0: A Vision for Safety," which was released in September 2017.
70 "Automated Driving Systems 2.0: A Vision for Safety" (September 2017).

- consumer education and training
- compliance with federal, state, and local laws

There is no legal requirement to prepare and publish this Voluntary Safety Self-Assessment, but the implication is that failure to provide it or to provide a complete version of it will attract scrutiny from NHTSA and might lead it to exercise its powers.

These powers include the power to determine that a vehicle contains a defect related to safety and require the manufacturer to remedy that defect by repairing the vehicle, replacing it, or refunding the purchase price.[71] This also prevents any further vehicles with the defect from being sold.[72] In order to determine whether there is a defect, NHTSA has powers to carry out inspections and investigations and request information from the manufacturer.

The prospect of NHTSA action is not an empty threat. As outlined in chapter 2, NHTSA investigated the Tesla autopilot mode in 2016 following a fatal crash and was prepared to take action had it not been satisfied as to the overall safety of the mode. Another good example of how this might work in practice for a driverless vehicle is provided by the recent case of Comma AI. This was a company that in October 2016 began promoting an upcoming electronic product called "Comma One," which it claimed could be retro-fitted to certain vehicles to allow them to operate in semiautonomous modes described as "lane keeping assist" and "adaptive cruise control." NHTSA was very concerned about the safety of this product. It ordered Comma AI to provide detailed information and answer a number of questions about the product, backed up by the threat of fines of up to $21,000 per day if the responses were not forthcoming.[73] As a result of this scrutiny, Comma AI decided not to release the product.

---

71 49 U.S.C. § 30118.
72 49 U.S.C. § 30112.
73 Special Order Directed to Comma AI, NHTSA, 27 October 2016, at https://www.scribd.com/document/329218929/2016-10-27-Special-Order-Directed-to-Comma-ai.

The fact that the US regulatory system does not (at present) contain prescriptive requirements for driverless systems, and instead utilises voluntary safety self-assessment, may have advantages (over systems —like the European system—that do) in allowing for the anticipated rapid development and improvement of driverless vehicles. For most of the last one hundred years, the pace of vehicle development and improvement has been limited by the need to design physical hardware and incorporate it into the production process.

For driverless vehicles, a lot of the most important advances will not be physical at all; they will be improvements to the software. This means that the vehicles can be improved much more quickly. But if improvements need to be assessed for self-certification or type approval (as in Europe), this could slow down the development process for driverless vehicles compared to a system where this is not required (as is currently the case in the US).

Even if the United States was to bring in prescriptive requirements for driverless vehicles, it is possible that the US system's reliance on self-certification rather than type approval by an independent agency, would still give the US system an edge in facilitating the improvement of technology. This is because self-certification can be done in-house without the need for third parties and approval processes, and so might be significantly swifter. Even though type approvals can often be obtained quite quickly for the traditional aspects of vehicles, this might not be the case for the approval of extremely complex driverless systems.

On the other hand, there may be concerns that the US system of self-certification is inferior to the European type-approval system when it comes to promoting safety. There is something reassuring about a system in which an independent vehicle-approving authority scrutinises every type or model and will not approve it until it is convinced that it meets standards and is safe. This seems highly preferable in many ways to a self-certification system, which is highly dependent on trusting manufacturers to scrutinise their own vehicles. But the US system has some safety advantages of its own.

Firstly, because it utilises post-certification scrutiny and market surveillance, it is not dependent on the independence of the vehicle-approving authorities and technical services providers. The European system is highly dependent on the independence of these entities. Furthermore, in the wake of the Volkswagen emissions scandal, the European Commission has voiced concerns about this independence. In 2015, Volkswagen admitted it had deliberately used "defeat devices" to allow its vehicles to fraudulently pass emission standards that they would otherwise have failed. A study by MIT and Harvard University[74] estimated that the excess emissions generated by the 482,000 vehicles exported to and operating in the United States from 2008 to 2015 will cause fifty-nine premature deaths. That is just in the United States. Presumably, the number of deaths at ground zero in Europe, where over eight million vehicles have been releasing excess emissions since at least 1998, will be much higher.

Documents leaked in 2016 indicated that European Commission officials had actually been warned in 2006 that a manufacturer was using defeat devices and did nothing.[75] Concern about this problem has led to the commission tabling a legislative proposal[76] in January 2016 to "modify the remuneration system to avoid financial links between technical services and manufacturers, which could lead to conflicts of interest and compromise the independence of testing." This legislative proposal has still not been adopted. If it was, it might help with this problem a bit, but it hard to see how it can change the fundamental issue of technical services being financially dependent on manufacturers.

Secondly, if the US system allows for faster adoption and development of safer driverless technology, then this could accelerate the safety dividend of driverless vehicles. As mentioned earlier, it is an open question as to whether the US system would allow for faster development. Whether it

---

74 S. Barrett, R. Speth, S. Eastham, I. Dedoussi, A. Ashok, R. Malina, and D. Keith, "Impact of the Volkswagon Emissions Control Defeat Device on US Public Health," *Environmental Research Letters* 10 no. 11 (29 October 2015).

75 Arthur Neslan, "European Commission Warned of Car Emissions Test Cheating, Five Years before VW Scandal," *Guardian*, 20 June 2016.

76 European Commission Press Release, Brussels, 27 January 2016, at http://europa.eu/rapid/press-release_IP-16-167_en.htm?locale=en.

does or not may largely depend on whether the United States continues to avoid having prescriptive requirements for driverless technology and whether self-certification really is significantly faster than type approval.

It is currently unclear whether the United States will adopt such prescriptive requirements for driverless technology. A recent bill that has just passed in the House of Representatives[77] would, if it also passes in the Senate, make the Voluntary Safety Self-Assessment into a mandatory requirement.

Whatever the merits of the US system, however, there are some pragmatic obstacles for US-certified driverless vehicles to enter New Zealand. To date, even though it is theoretically possible for vehicles to enter service onto New Zealand roads on the strength of compliance with US standards, this is rare, even for US-manufactured vehicles. The prosaic reason for this is related to the fact that New Zealanders drive on the left-hand side of the road and need vehicles with the steering wheel on the right-hand side. When a US manufacturer develops a new model of vehicle, it will develop a US version to comply with the US standards and sell in the United States. This version will have the steering wheel on the left-hand side so that it can drive on the right-hand side of American roads. It is of no use in New Zealand and would not be able to be certified in large numbers to enter service on our roads.

If New Zealanders want to import a US vehicle, they will have to wait to see if the US manufacturer develops a right-hand-drive version of the vehicle for a left-hand-driving country, such as the United Kingdom or Australia. And this version will also be modified to meet the different standards of the target market. If a US manufacturer did make and self-certify a right-hand-drive variant of the US version of a model, then it could be imported into New Zealand. But it is almost certainly not worth it for a manufacturer to do this because there are no sizable markets that would accept it. New Zealand is small, and, in any case, New Zealand will accept

---

77 Safely Ensuring Lives Future Deployment and Research in Vehicle Evolution Act (known as the SELF DRIVE act), https://www.congress.gov/115/bills/hr3388/BILLS-115hr3388rfs.pdf.

vehicles built to comply with other standards. And though many driverless vehicles are likely to eventually have no steering wheel, the first driverless vehicles probably will have steering wheels and other driver controls. This is for two reasons. Firstly, they may need these controls because they might not be able to operate as a driverless vehicle in all situations. Secondly, the vehicle standards in all countries—as currently drafted—require these controls.

D. The Australian Motor Vehicle Approval System

Australia is a signatory to the 1958 convention and so uses a type-approval system similar to that used in Europe. Vehicles can be certified for the Australian market against the Australian Design Rules (ADR).[78] It is possible for testing to be carried out in Australia, but what currently happens is that manufacturers send their own testing data to the Vehicle Safety Standards Branch of the Australian Department of Infrastructure and Development, which then uses this to decide whether to issue a type approval. Large portions of the text of UNECE regulations are incorporated into the ADR, so manufacturers often have the option of using a UNECE approval to show compliance with a particular ADR.

The ADR are less prescriptive than the UNECE regulations with respect to driverless technology. The ADR equivalents of UNECE 79 (which governs steering systems) are ADR 10/02 and ADR 42/04. In their content, these standards are more like the FMVSS in that they do not contain any prescriptive provisions that pose a barrier to driverless systems. This means that—in theory—a new driverless vehicle could be approved relatively easily in Australia.

The National Transport Commission of Australia has recently released a policy paper,[79] which recommends that Australia should—for the time

---

78 https://infrastructure.gov.au/roads/motor/design/index.aspx.

79 Assuring the safety of automated vehicles (November 2017), http://www.ntc.gov.au/Media/Reports/(A19CA1B2-EDEE-7167-23AC-F1B305100F30).pdf.

being—refrain from introducing any prescriptive requirements for driverless vehicles. It instead recommends introducing a system of mandatory self-certification. This would be similar to the current US system. The important difference would be that in the United States, manufacturers are merely encouraged to publish a voluntary safety self-assessment, whereas this would be mandatory in Australia. And the statement of compliance would also need to be approved by Australian authorities before vehicles could enter service. One of the main reasons for this difference is that Australia does not have the equivalent of NHTSA's post-certification scrutiny and market surveillance. This makes up-front scrutiny more important.

The National Transport Commission's policy paper indicates that Australia aims to have "end-to-end regulation in place by 2020."

E. The Japanese Motor Vehicle Approval System

Japan is also a signatory to the 1958 convention and uses a type-approval system. Its system is currently closer to the European system than the Australian system in that it does contain some prescriptive requirements that apply to driverless systems. It is currently very unclear as to whether and when a fully driverless vehicle could be type approved in Japan.

F. The Prospects for the Entry of Driverless Vehicles onto New Zealand Roads

It is technically possible for driverless vehicles to be certified to enter onto and operate legally on New Zealand roads right now.

There is currently nothing to stop a driverless vehicle from being self-certified in the United States and then being certified for entry onto New Zealand roads. But, in practice, because of the fact that US certified vehicles will be left-hand drive, New Zealand is unlikely to see any US certified driverless vehicles in the near future (with the possible exception of vehicles that don't have a steering wheel or other controls—more on this later in this chapter).

This practical barrier does not exist for driverless vehicles that have been type-approved in Australia. As with the United States, there is nothing to stop a driverless vehicle from being type-approved in Australia. But unlike vehicles self-certified for the US market, Australian type-approved vehicles will be right-hand drive, so there is also nothing to stop them being certified for entry onto New Zealand roads.

As for Europe and Japan, it does not currently appear to be possible for driverless vehicles to be type-approved in those jurisdictions. But it is possible for vehicles that have driverless capability, in terms of their hardware but not in terms of their software, to be type-approved in Europe or Japan (or Australia or the United States for that matter). They could then be certified for entry to New Zealand roads and then receive a software update to activate their driverless capabilities. Examples of such vehicles could include the latest Audi A8, and the Tesla Models S, X and 3. The Tesla Models S and X are already on New Zealand roads, having gained entry in reliance upon their European type-approval.

Software updates to activate a vehicle's driverless capability after it has entered service on to New Zealand roads would not appear to affect the ability of these vehicles to continue operating legally under New Zealand law. This might seem a surprising conclusion. As noted, New Zealand's Land Transport Rule: Steering Systems 2001 requires the steering systems of a vehicle on the road to comply with the relevant approved vehicle standards. If a vehicle has gained certification to enter service on to New Zealand roads by relying upon its type approval against European standards (and the UN standards incorporated within them) and it no longer complies with those standards, then how can it still comply with Steering Systems 2001? The answer lies in the fact that Steering Systems 2001 recognises[80] compliance with any of the relevant approved vehicle standards from Europe, the United States, Australia, Japan, or the United Nations. So even if the software activation of a vehicle's driverless capability means that it no longer complies with the relevant European/UN standard on

---

80 See rules 2.1–2.3.

steering (UNECE79), it can still comply with the relevant Australian standards (ADR 10/02 and ADR 42/04), which—as noted earlier—contain no prescriptive requirements pertaining to driverless systems.

For anyone interested in seeing New Zealand receiving driverless vehicles on our roads sooner rather than later, the current situation could be viewed as desirable. It could see New Zealand receiving driverless vehicles before Australia, Europe, or Japan and at the same or a similar time to the United States. The potential route would be if the manufacturers of the first driverless vehicles get versions of these vehicles (without the driverless software) approved in Europe, Australia, or Japan, and then these vehicles receive driverless software updates after they have been certified for entry onto the road in New Zealand. The other route would be if a driverless vehicle with its driverless software is type-approved in Australia and then certified for New Zealand roads. This latter route is possibly less likely in practice because manufacturers would have less incentive to manufacture vehicles for the Australian market due to (i) its smaller size and (ii) the fact that Australia has decided to impose an additional regulatory restriction on top of type-approval by requiring the approval of a statement of compliance with principles based driverless vehicle safety criteria.

We shouldn't underestimate the extent to which well-meaning safety assurance measures in Europe, Japan, and Australia might delay the introduction of driverless vehicles. Introduction in Europe and Japan will have to wait until their regulations are amended to remove current blanket restrictions on driverless vehicles and replace them with provisions that allow driverless vehicles provided they meet prescriptive requirements. We do not know how long this might take.

Even once they have been amended to allow driverless vehicles to be type-approved, it is uncertain how long it would take for vehicles to obtain type approval. The systems used by driverless vehicles are extremely complex, and there isn't really anyone outside of the companies developing them who understands enough about these systems to judge their safety and efficacy. Even the experts within the companies developing the systems would be hard pressed to fully understand the systems being developed by their competitors. If the vehicle approval authorities in Europe or Japan are required to vouch for the safety of these systems, it may be necessary to take them on a long journey to get them up to speed on how they work. There is no guarantee that the staff in the approval authorities will ever get up to speed, and how can they vouch for and approve a system they do not understand?

Even if there were staff or contractors within the approval authorities who were capable of learning how the systems work in a reasonable amount of time, many companies will be extremely reluctant to divulge the information needed to gain this understanding. Manufacturers are currently engaged in a race to gain the lead in driverless vehicle systems, and they will be wary of the risk they may lose proprietary information to their competitors. There is a serious possibility that some companies would prefer not to risk their trade secrets and would choose not to put some (or any) of their driverless systems through the European or Japanese type-approval processes. It might be better for them to concentrate on the US market, leaving countries that depend on type-approval of driverless systems out in the cold.

From the perspective of safety, the current situation in New Zealand is more of a mixed blessing. While it still provides assurance as to the mechanical and other physical aspects of driverless vehicles, it does nothing to provide assurance about the safety of the driverless systems themselves. Other jurisdictions have mechanisms to try to ensure a level of safety for driverless vehicles. The United States has its voluntary safety self-assessment, backed by possible regulatory action if the authorities have concerns about safety. Australia will have the mandatory statement of compliance that needs to be approved before the vehicles are allowed on the roads. And Europe and Japan will require driverless vehicles to meet prescriptive type-approval standards with respect to their driverless functions.

The New Zealand Ministry of Transport has collaborated extensively with Australia in the development of policy options and is well apprised of the pros and cons, but the New Zealand government has yet to make any decisions about implementing mechanisms to ensure the safety of driverless vehicles.

It could be argued that this is a good thing for safety. Conventional vehicles are hardly paragons of safety. Their vulnerability to human error results in a constant stream of accidents, causing untold misery, including an annual death toll of over three hundred people in New Zealand alone. Even if the imposition of additional safety assurance mechanisms provides greater reassurance that vehicles are safe, this may still not be worth it if the cost is to delay the introduction and improvement of driverless vehicles. As we saw in chapter 2, there is already some real-world evidence (in the form of the NHTSA report into the Tesla crash, which noted the 40 percent reduction in crash rates after the introduction of autopilot technology in Tesla vehicles[81]) that driverless vehicles can be safer than human-driven vehicles.

From the perspective of the economy and jobs, the current situation could be argued to be quite positive. If New Zealand has a more receptive legal environment to the entry of driverless vehicles onto its roads, then this might be expected to encourage more investment by domestic and overseas companies. This could have positive economic results far beyond driverless vehicles. As noted in chapter 1, these vehicles are the first mass application of artificial intelligence to the physical world. Economies that are receptive to driverless vehicles have a chance to catch the coming wave of robotic automation, and ride it to greater prosperity.

There is, however, a potential fly in the ointment in terms of New Zealand's current receptiveness to driverless vehicles. New Zealand may not be very receptive to steering wheel-less driverless vehicles. As discussed, the very first driverless vehicles are likely to have steering wheels, pedals, and other driver controls. This is partly because they will not be

---

81 Kareem Habib, Investigation PE 16-007, 19 January 2017, National Highway Traffic Safety Administration.

able to drive themselves in every situation and partly because the standards to which they need to comply require these controls.

But it may not be that long before we start seeing vehicles without such controls. As mentioned in chapter 2, GM announced in January 2018 that it intends to begin mass-producing driverless vehicles without such controls in 2019.[82] And as mentioned in chapter 3, driverless cargo pods without driver controls or even seats (such as the R1 being tested by Nuro) are being developed for imminent deployment on US roads. The fact that these US manufactured vehicles do not have steering wheels or other controls makes it both easier and harder for them to enter New Zealand. It makes it easier because it removes the left-hand/right-hand drive problem, and so eliminates the need for a right-hand-drive variant to be developed for type approval in a jurisdiction that drives on the left side. It makes it harder because vehicles without steering wheels and other driver controls do not comply with the current FMVSS, so cannot obtain the self-certification necessary to be legal on US roads and (by extension) New Zealand roads. Ultimately, the prospects for such a vehicle entering New Zealand will depend on the legal method by which its manufacturer gets it to operate on US roads legally despite its non-compliance with the FMVSS.

If manufacturers petition NHTSA to amend the FMVSS to remove requirements for steering wheels and other controls, then prospects for entry to New Zealand are good. NHTSA is currently seeking public comment to identify any regulatory barriers in the FMVSS and is specifically interested in amendments to allow vehicles that do not have steering wheels and other controls. So amendments to the FMVSS are a real possibility. If these amendments eventuate then this would allow manufacturers to self-certify steering wheel-less vehicles, and they would then be able to enter New Zealand off the back of that certification.

---

82 Neal Boudette, "G.M. Says Its Driverless Cars Could Be in Fleets by Next Year," *New York Times*, 12 January 2018.

Alternatively, manufacturers might seek and obtain from US Secretary of Transportation an exemption[83] from the FMVSS requirements. These exemptions may be granted by the Secretary if he or she considers that the exemption would not result in a lower level of safety. If this is the method by which steering wheel-less driverless vehicles are allowed on to US roads, then this would not bode well for the entry of such vehicles to New Zealand. New Zealand law does not recognize exemptions to FMVSS. In the eyes of the New Zealand system, a vehicle either complies with the FMVSS, or it does not. The method that GM is currently pursuing for its planned roll-out of a driverless ride-hailing fleet in 2019 is an exemption, and—at this point—it would appear that exemptions are the more likely means by which steering wheel-less driverless vehicles will be allowed on to US roads.

Recommendations

New Zealand's current system will continue to provide assurance that the non-driverless mechanical and other physical aspects of vehicles are safe by ensuring that no vehicle can be certified for entry onto the road without these aspects being subject to type-approval in Europe, Australia, or Japan, or self-certification in the United States.

At the same time, it is not desirable that New Zealand's system has the potential to allow driverless vehicles to operate while having no deliberate mechanisms to try to ensure the safety of their driverless systems. New Zealand may derive some safety assurance from the Australian system of mandatory self-certification and the US system of voluntary safety self-assessment. But these systems will be assessing the safety of the vehicles for Australian and US conditions. They will not take into account whether there has been sufficient mapping of New Zealand roads and testing carried out under New Zealand conditions. Furthermore, as noted earlier, it is theoretically possible for an Australian type-approved vehicle to be

---

83 Under 49 USC 30113.

certified for New Zealand roads before it has been through the mandatory self-certification system in Australia.

New Zealand has the option of addressing this by instituting a similar process to that planned in Australia, where manufacturers will be required to produce a mandatory statement of compliance that needs to be approved before the vehicles are allowed on the roads.

My view is that New Zealand would be better served by adopting a voluntary safety self-assessment along the lines of the US model. The elements to be covered in this assessment could be modelled on the NHTSA's automated vehicles policy. This would enable manufacturers who have submitted such an assessment in the United States to reuse large parts of it for the New Zealand assessment, while including additional sections to explain why the vehicle (or the software update being offered in New Zealand) was also considered to be safe under New Zealand's different roads and other conditions. If it cannot do this, then New Zealand has its own product recall powers that could be brought into play. Under section 32 of the Fair Trading Act 1986 the Minister of Consumer Affairs may require the supplier to recall goods if it appears to the Minister that a reasonably foreseeable use (including misuse) of the goods (or the software) supplied by the supplier will, or may, cause injury to any person. Another enforcement mechanism would be for the New Zealand Transport Agency (NZTA) to issue general guidance about driverless capable vehicles to vehicle inspectors that would result in refusals to issue a warrant of fitness under the Land Transport Act 1998.

Another undesirable feature of New Zealand's system is that it will not admit vehicles that have gained access to US roads through exemptions to the FMVSS. This means that New Zealand could miss out on any chance of being an early adopter with respect to vehicles such as GM's upcoming ride hailing fleet vehicles, even though the exemptions cannot be granted without the US Secretary of Transportation being satisfied as to their safety. I am also therefore recommending an amendment to rule 6.4(2) of Land Transport Rule: Vehicle Standards Compliance 2002, to allow such exempted vehicles to be certified for entry on to New Zealand roads.

Recommendation 3

Adopt a voluntary safety self-assessment model along the lines of the US model. Manufacturers would be encouraged to publish this assessment. If there are still concerns about the safety of vehicles, then regulatory action under the Fair Trading Act 1986 or the Land Transport Act 1998 should be considered.

Recommendation 4

Amend rule 6.4(2) of Land Transport Rule: Vehicle Standards Compliance 2002, to allow exempted vehicles to be certified for entry on New Zealand roads.

6.4(2)   For the purposes of 6.4(1)(c), a vehicle complies with an applicable requirement if it:

(a)   complied with an approved vehicle standard in that applicable requirement, <u>or was exempt from that standard,</u> when manufactured or modified; and

Civil Liability for Property Damage

ven if driverless vehicles are as superior to human drivers as is hoped, they will not be perfect—especially not at first. They will still make mistakes and cause accidents. It will be important that the law is clear about who is liable for the cost of remedying the damage caused by these accidents.

A. Current Legal Situation

Before we examine whether some reform would be desirable, it is necessary to look at the current legal situation with (i) traditional vehicles, (ii) semiautonomous vehicles that require driver supervision, and (iii) fully autonomous vehicles that do not require supervision.

A1. Liability with Traditional Vehicles

When a traditional vehicle driven by a human collides with another vehicle or something else and causes damage, there will usually be questions about who should have to pay for the resulting losses.

Rather than letting the losses lie where they fall, there will often be one party who is considered to be at fault and is liable to pay for some or all of the losses of other parties.

That other party would usually be another road user, but other parties could also be liable, including the person responsible for ensuring a vehicle was properly maintained, a mechanic who repaired or serviced a vehicle, or the manufacturer. This shifting of losses is done in the name of fairness and to incentivise prudent behaviour.

There will also usually be insurance companies involved. When the liability of various parties is discussed in the rest of the chapter, it should go without saying that in most cases, it is really the liability of the party's insurance company that is at issue.

The other important thing to remember is that New Zealand is somewhat of a special case in that tortious actions for personal injury are barred by section 317 of the Accident Compensation Act 2001, and compensation is instead payable under the scheme set up by that act. There is no cover for certain mental injury claims and a few other special cases where tortious claims can still be made. Exemplary damages also are still recoverable, as they seek to punish the wrongdoer, not to compensate the victim. However, for most cases of motor accidents in New Zealand, we only really need to be concerned about liability for property losses. The rest of this chapter is solely concerned with liability for property loss. Chapter 7 deals with personal injury and accident compensation.

Liability of Other Road Users

The basis for the liability of road users in an accident is the law of tort and the duty of care that road users owe each other. When someone breaches this duty, he or she may be liable in negligence.

This liability seems to be so ancient and self-evident that there is no foundational case law to which one can refer. When you look at negligence more broadly, the common law is filled with examples of cases where the courts have struggled to determine whether a duty of care exists and how far it extends. But these are the exceptions that made it to court. The majority of cases are open and shut with regard to the duty of care and do not make it to the courts. The liability of road users is a case in point. As noted in New Zealand's foremost textbook on the law of torts,[84] "The existence or ambit of a duty in any particular case is usually well established and is not a live issue. For example, there can be no

---

84 Stephen Todd et al., *The Law of Torts in New Zealand*, 7th Edition (Thomson Reuters, 2016), 157–158.

argument about whether a driver owes a duty of care to other road users to take care in his or her driving."

A leading textbook *Aitiyah's Accidents, Compensation and the Law*[85] simply asserts the reality of this liability as follows.

> Legal liability for negligence resulting in road accidents has been recognized certainly since the seventeenth century and perhaps earlier. There has never been any doubt that those using the highways are under a duty of care in so doing, and the legal position today is plain: any person using the roads, whether as a motorist, pedestrian or cyclist, will be liable if, by positive action, that person negligently causes physical injury to anyone else. A lawyer would scarcely ever waste time in an ordinary road accident case by inquiring whether the defendant owed a duty of care to the claimant. This would simply be taken for granted.

When there is a collision between two vehicles in New Zealand, the basic approach in determining liability is to investigate whether one of the parties has failed to take reasonable care. This may be established by evidence that they have breached some element of the road code[86] or other law relating to the road.[87] Did they fail to give way? Were they speeding?

If such a breach has occurred, the next question is whether it caused or contributed to the accident. For example, one of the parties involved in an accident may have failed to maintain their vehicle in an appropriate condition,[88] but unless this contributed to the accident, it will not have any bearing on liability.

---

85 Peter Cane, *Atiyah's Accidents, Compensation and the Law*, 7th edition (Cambridge University Press, 2006), 70–71.
86 Set out in the Land Transport (Road User) Rule 2004.
87 For example, driving recklessly, as described in section 7 of the Land Transport Act 1998.
88 Clause 8.9 of Land Transport (Road User) Rule 2004 requires the operator to keep the vehicle in an appropriate condition, and regulations 3 and 4 and schedule 1 of the Land

Even if there is a technical breach by one of the parties, it is still possible that the party will not be liable if the breach is not his or her fault. For example, if a driver failed to give way but this was due to sudden fainting caused by an undiagnosed medical condition, then this is not the driver's fault and the driver cannot be liable.[89] In a case like this, damage will just be left to lie where it falls. No one is responsible. For the other party—whose vehicle was damaged by the fainting driver's vehicle—it is just as if their vehicle was damaged by a falling tree or other random act of nature. Another example might be a sudden gust of wind that blew a vehicle into the wrong lane and into the path of another vehicle. It would have to be an extreme wind though. As explained by Atiyah, "a natural causal factor will be treated as the cause of an event in preference to tortious human conduct only if it was sufficiently out of the ordinary and improbable that it could be described as 'totally unexpected' or a 'sheer coincidence.'"[90]

Liability of Owners/Operators

The operator of a vehicle has a legal duty to keep the vehicle in a condition appropriate to the level required for the issue of a warrant of fitness.[91] If the operator breaches this duty by failing to keep the vehicle in an appropriate condition and if this causes a mechanical failure (e.g., a brake failure), which in turn causes the vehicle to crash, then the operator may be liable for any resulting property damage. But not all operators will necessarily be liable under these circumstances. If an operator who took reasonable care to maintain the vehicle is to be held liable, then this amounts to an imposition of strict liability. In 1923, the Court of Appeal in

---

Transport (Offences and Penalties) Regulations 1999 specify a breach as a regular offence and an infringement offence.

89 *Robinson v Glover* [1952] NZLR 669.

90 Peter Cane, *Atiyah's Accidents, Compensation and the Law*, 7th edition (Cambridge University Press, 2006), 121.

91 Clause 8.9 of Land Transport (Road User) Rule 2004 requires the operator to keep the vehicle in an appropriate condition, and regulations 3 and 4 and schedule 1 of the Land Transport (Offences and Penalties) Regulations 1999 specify a breach as a regular offence and an infringement offence.

England refused to impose strict liability for the breach of a statutory duty for breach of Ministry of Transport regulations relating to the construction and use of motor vehicles.[92] The court considered that Parliament did not intend to confer a civil remedy for the breach of these regulations. The same argument could be made in New Zealand. The legal duty to maintain a vehicle in an appropriate condition already has criminal penalties attached to its breach. For someone to succeed in an action claiming compensation for damages caused by someone's failure to keep a vehicle in an appropriate condition, it may therefore not be enough to merely show that that they had failed to maintain the vehicle. It may be necessary to also show that the operator did not make reasonable efforts to maintain the vehicle.

Liability of Warrant of Fitness Inspectors

A warrant of fitness agent who is inspecting a vehicle for the purposes of determining whether to certify it for a warrant of fitness may be liable under some circumstances. The law states that the agent must not certify a vehicle if he or she has any reason to believe it does not comply with any of the relevant land transport rules.[93] If the agent does certify a vehicle for a warrant, despite having reason to believe that it does not comply, and as a result, the vehicle suffers from a mechanical failure that causes an accident, then that agent could be liable for any resulting property damage.

As with the duty to keep a vehicle in an appropriate condition, there may be an argument that a strict breach alone may not be enough for liability, and it may be necessary to show that the agent was negligent (although it is a bit difficult to see how an agent who had reason to believe a vehicle did not comply and nevertheless certified it could not be negligent).

---

92 *Phillips v. Britannia Hygienic Laundry* [1923] 2 KB 832.

93 All of the relevant Land Transport Rules pertaining to the different aspects of vehicles contain this requirement. See, for example, rule 4.4 of Land Transport Rule: Light-Vehicle Brakes 2002.

Liability of Repairers/Modifiers

A person who is repairing or modifying a vehicle must ensure that the repair or modification does not prevent the vehicle from complying with any of the relevant Land Transport rules.[94] If the repair or modification does prevent compliance and as a result the vehicle suffers from a mechanical failure that causes an accident, then that person could be liable for any resulting property damage. But again, it may not be enough just to show that the repair or modification prevented compliance. It may also be necessary to show a negligent lack of care or professionalism.

Liability of Manufacturers

Motor vehicles that are supplied to a consumer are, like other consumer goods, governed by the Consumer Guarantees Act 1993. Section 6 of that Act confers a guarantee that a vehicle is of acceptable quality. If it isn't, then a consumer who acquires the vehicle for his or her own use has rights of redress against the supplier and the manufacturer. So, for example, suppose a vehicle had defective brakes, and this was due to its design or manufacture (not neglect by the owner/operator). This may mean that the vehicle is not of acceptable quality under section 6, and the consumer may be entitled to some sort of redress from the manufacturer, such as free repair or even replacement of the whole vehicle.[95] This entitlement is not limited to the first owner of the vehicle. Subsequent owners have the same entitlement.[96]

If the vehicle crashes as a result of the defective brakes, then the owner is, in theory, able to claim for damage to the vehicle and any other losses that result (on the basis that such loss was reasonably foreseeable

---

94 See, for example, rules 4.2 and 4.3 of Land Transport Rule: Light-Vehicle Brakes 2002.

95 Section 25(a) of the Consumer Guarantees Act 1993 provides that a consumer has a right of redress against a manufacturer of goods when those goods fail to comply with the statutory guarantee as to acceptable quality. Section 27(2) sets out repair or replacement as possible remedies.

96 Section 27 grants the rights of redress to any person who acquires the vehicle from or through a consumer.

as liable to result from defective brakes).[97] There do not appear to be any cases in New Zealand where somebody has ever made such a claim under the Consumer Guarantees Act against a manufacturer. This is possibly a testament to the quality of vehicles. Or it could be due to the difficulty and expense of determining that a crash was due to a brake or other mechanical failure or that the failure was due to the manufacturer not producing a vehicle of acceptable quality (rather than being due to, say, poor maintenance). When most people have insurance, it is easier and cheaper for everyone concerned for the insurance companies to pay. But the possibility is there for insurance companies or other parties to shift the liability to the manufacturer in appropriate cases.

However, that possibility only exists for the owner of the defective vehicle (and their insurer). Any other parties who suffer loss as a result of the defective brakes (e.g., the owner of another vehicle into which the vehicle with defective brakes crashed) are unable to claim under the Consumer Guarantees Act. That Act only confers rights on the person who owns the vehicle.

Other parties would not be able to claim against the owner or the driver of the defective vehicle (it was not their fault it was defective). If they wish to claim against the manufacturer, they must make out a case under the general law of negligence. This will be governed by the famous "neighbour principle" as set out by Lord Atkin in *Donoghue v Stevenson*[98]:

> By Scots and English law alike a manufacturer of products, which he sells in such a form as to show that he intends them to reach the ultimate consumer in the form in which they left him with no reasonable possibility of intermediate examination, and with the knowledge that the absence of reasonable care in the preparation or putting up of the products will result in an injury to

---

97 Section 27(1)(a) allows damages for any loss or damage resulting from the failure that was reasonably foreseeable as liable to result from the failure.
98 *Donoghue v Stevenson* [1932] AC 562 (HL) at 599.

the consumer's life or property, owes a duty to the consumer to take that reasonable care.

In our example of a vehicle with brakes that were defective due to a problem with the design or manufacturing process, it would be fairly straightforward to show that the manufacturer owes a duty to take reasonable care. It should be obvious to any manufacturer that a vehicle with defective brakes will likely result in injury. And this duty is owed not only to owners of the defective vehicle but anyone who ought reasonably to have been foreseen as likely to be affected by the defect (e.g., other road users into which the vehicle crashes).[99] Whether the manufacturer has in fact failed to take reasonable care and is therefore liable will depend on the exact circumstances. It will be necessary for the plaintiff to show, on the balance of probabilities, that the defect was the result of negligence on the part of the manufacturer. This could be difficult if the plaintiff has little information about how the defect came into existence. The plaintiff may be able rely on the doctrine of res ipsa loquitur, whereby the "facts speak for themselves" and an inference of negligence can be drawn when there is an accident that normally could not happen without negligence on behalf of the manufacturer.

In George v Eagle Air Services Ltd,[100] the manufacturer was held liable when a plane crashed during landing. The court considered that aircraft do not ordinarily crash, and the defendant had failed to displace the inference of negligence. An example where a manufacturer did manage to displace this inference is provided by Web v Cassidy.[101] Here, the manufacturer of a coach was not liable for an accident caused by the failure of an axle. This was because the axle had been supplied by a reputable firm, and it was not possible for the manufacturer to detect the defect within the axle. So for our example of defective brakes, if the reason for

---

99 Stennet v Hancock [1939] 2 All ER 578; Lambert v Lewis [1982] AC 225 (HL).
100 George v Eagle Air Services Ltd. [2009] UKPC 21, [2009] WLR 2133; K Williams (2009) 125 LQR 567.
101 Web v Cassidy (1907) 27 NZLR 489 (SC).

the defect in the brakes was that the manufacturer used a subcomponent from a reputable supplier and that subcomponent had an undetectable defect, then the manufacturer may not be liable.

A2. Liability with Semiautonomous Vehicles that Require Driver Supervision

Here we are talking about a situation where a manufacturer has provided a semiautonomous mode for a vehicle, which it says requires driver supervision at all times. This would include advanced modes like Mercedes' Intelligent Drive or Tesla's autopilot, as well as more basic modes, such as lane keeping and even cruise control. If the vehicle "makes a mistake" while using such a mode (e.g., it does not give way to another vehicle that has the right of way) and causes an accident, then, in most cases, it is logical that the driver should still be held responsible. The driver had been put on notice by the manufacturer that the vehicle mode cannot necessarily be trusted and needs to be supervised. So the legally relevant mistake here is actually by the driver for not using the product as directed. The driver was not paying attention and did not notice and correct the mistake by the vehicle.

Having said this, there are examples of a product not being used as directed and yet the manufacturer was nevertheless held liable for the consequences of its failure because the use was reasonably foreseeable. In *Hill v James Crowe Ltd.*,[102] the manufacturer was liable when a badly nailed packing case collapsed and injured a man who had been standing on it. The crate was not designed for a person to stand on, but it was reasonably foreseeable that someone might stand on it and that injury might result if it was badly nailed. Similarly, it is foreseeable that a driver may come to place too much trust in a seemingly competent semiautonomous vehicle and stop paying adequate attention. It is not difficult to imagine

---

102 See *Hill v James Crowe Ltd* [1978] 1 All ER 812.

that a court could hold a manufacturer liable in certain circumstances.[103] This is made much less likely, however, by the mechanisms that manufacturers are increasingly using to guard against this kind of complacency by drivers, such as sensors in the steering to detect hands on the wheel and cameras to observe the driver's eyes.

There may also be situations where it would be illogical to blame the driver at all. If a driver assistance mode was to malfunction and cause the vehicle to suddenly lurch into the other lane or do something else that the driver could not reasonably be expected to counteract, then that should be treated as a defect for which the manufacturer could be liable (in much the same way as they might be liable for faulty brakes as explained earlier).

A3. Liability with Fully Autonomous Vehicles that Do Not Require Supervision

Here we are talking about vehicles for which the manufacturer has provided a mode that it says can operate without driver supervision in at least some circumstances. As outlined in chapter 3, the most likely such mode—at first—may be a highway driving mode (like that allegedly possessed by the latest Audi A8), where the driver can set the vehicle to take over the driving completely until a preset point (such as the off-ramp) or until the vehicle strikes conditions beyond its capabilities (such as thick fog).

Suppose such a vehicle was to make a mistake, such as running into the vehicle in front of it, while operating in a mode like this. It is highly likely that the courts would consider it to be analogous to the example explored earlier where a traditional vehicle crashes because of a design or manufacturing defect (such as faulty brakes). It should be obvious to any manufacturer that if it offers, for sale or use, a driverless vehicle that

---

103 This might be an example of the "in solidum" rule of liability, where two persons (the manufacturer and the driver/user) contribute to indivisible damage and are both fully liable. In this case, a plaintiff can pursue either of the parties for the full extent of their loss.

sometimes makes mistakes when being used as directed, then injury to property is likely to result. It may well be that manufacturers would pro-actively assume liability for these kinds of accidents. They are likely to be confident enough in their product that this would not be a huge financial risk. Assuming this responsibility voluntarily would also be a shrewd move to increase consumer confidence in and public acceptance of their prod-uct. And a number of companies, such as Volvo, Mercedes, and Google, have already made public statements about assuming liability.[104]

There may be subtleties to the proposition that the manufacturer will always be liable for the mistakes of their vehicles. What if the driver/operator had directed the vehicle to operate outside of its "operational design domain"? For example, the driver/operator might have directed the vehicle to drive through geographical areas that the manufacturer had warned against (perhaps because these areas had not been mapped, tested, or validated by the manufacturer). In this case, the vehicle would not be being used as directed and it might be logical to hold the driver/operator responsible instead. On the other hand, it is possible that the courts might be inclined to consider that it was reasonably foreseeable that drivers/operators may "misuse" the vehicle in this way.[105] They might consider that the manufacturer should have ensured that the vehicle would "refuse" to use the self-driving mode outside of its competent geographical domain, and so the manufacturer is liable *in solidum* with the user (although it is probably more likely that they would regard it as wholly the fault of the operator). It may be that manufacturers would in fact ensure their vehicles cannot be misused in this way, and so ques-tions like this will not arise. Or manufacturers might judge that vehicles shouldn't refuse instructions, even when they take it outside of its com-petent domain. There might be situations where it is very important to be able to use the driverless mode. For example, the driver/operator might

---

104 Jim Gorzelany, "Volvo Will Accept Liability for Its Self-Driving Cars," *Forbes*, 9 October 2015.

105 *Hill v James Crowe Ltd.* [1978] 1 All ER 812.

be having a heart attack, be unable to drive, and need the vehicle to drive to the nearest hospital, which happens to be outside of the vehicle's competent geographical domain. Something like this actually happened in 2016 when a Tesla Model X driver suffered a pulmonary embolism and instructed autopilot to drive him thirty-five kilometres to the nearest hospital.[106] That driver credited his vehicle for saving his life. So the manufacturer might convincingly argue that the most responsible policy would be to warn the operator/driver when an instruction is taking the vehicle outside of its operational design domain but not refuse to implement the instruction. The operator/driver is in the best position to judge whether something is important enough to override the warning but should also bear the responsibility if something goes wrong, especially if the override was for a frivolous reason.

The liability of a manufacturer may also vary depending on the business model being used for the deployment of vehicles. Another likely early manifestation of driverless vehicles is the app-based ride-sharing fleets described in chapter 3. The vehicles could be owned by a single company, a mixture of companies, individuals lending their vehicles to the fleet when not using them, or a mixture of all of these. Under this model, a single company would assume responsibility for the management of a fleet of driverless vehicles providing taxi services requested by members of the public using phone apps or other technological means. This management company would be in the best position to ensure that the vehicles are operated safely and within their operational design domain, so it would probably enter into a contract with all the other parties to indemnify them and assume the ultimate liability for any accidents caused by the vehicles.

There is another way of looking at the liability of a manufacturer that could be used to argue against any liability. All of the previous is based on an assumption that a manufacturer would be liable whenever its vehicle

---

106 David Morris, "Tesla Autopilot Drives Owner to Hospital during Pulmonary Embolism," *Fortune*, 9 August 2016.

does something that would be regarded as negligent if a human had been driving. But it is arguable that this is not the test. The manufacturer's liability is not based directly on what the vehicle does. It is derived from product liability. It relies on saying that the manufacturer that designs and constructs a vehicle that has made a mistake has committed a negligent act during this design and construction. There is a potential problem with that characterisation. If a manufacturer has developed a driverless vehicle that is safer than a regular vehicle driven by the best human driver (which is likely to be the case; otherwise, the manufacturer would not be promoting it, and the NZTA would be unlikely to tolerate its use on public roads) then that vehicle is a marvel of human ingenuity. Crashes caused by this vehicle would be a rare occurrence, and its development would rank among the most impressive accomplishments of our species to date. It seems a bit of a stretch then to conclude that because the vehicle was not 100 percent infallible, the manufacturer has been negligent. This would be tantamount to imposing strict liability on the manufacturer for any accidents caused by their vehicle.

This is not to say that it wouldn't be a good idea from a policy perspective to hold manufacturers liable on a strict liability basis when their vehicles cause accidents. There is broad international support for this proposition.[107] But New Zealand does not have strict liability for product liability cases. Other countries have instituted strict liability regimes when a manufacturer's product fails and causes damage. But New Zealand has not. This is probably due to the fact that personal injuries—which are usually by far the most expensive portion of the losses caused by a product failure—are covered by ACC. There is not nearly as much incentive or reason to set up such a regime.[108] You have to either show negligence or show that the vehicle was not of acceptable quality in terms of section 6

---

107 For example, see the discussion of Ethical Guidelines 10 and 11 in the German Ethics Code for Automated and Connected Driving by Luetge Christoph. *The German Ethics Code for Automated and Connected Driving, Philos. Technol.* 30 (2017): 547–558.

108 See Stephen Todd et al., *The Law of Torts in New Zealand*, 7th Edition (Thomson Reuters, 2016), 345.

of the Consumer Guarantees Act 1993. As discussed earlier, this might end up being an academic question, if manufacturers decide to proactively assume responsibility. Even if this is what happens, it is still important that the background liability of manufacturers has a solid and logical legal foundation.

B. Is the Current Legal Situation Desirable?

The current law seems well placed to allocate liability appropriately in the case of semiautonomous vehicles that require driver supervision. In the main, the driver should still be responsible, and the courts are well equipped to ascertain those cases where the manufacturer should be exclusively liable or liable *in solidum* with the user.

But it is less than ideal when it comes to allocating liability in a situation where a fully autonomous vehicle is responsible for a collision. The main problem is that the courts will be forced to either:(i) impose liability on the manufacturer of the vehicle responsible for the collision on the basis that the manufacturer has been negligent or has produced a product that is not of acceptable quality, even though it may be quite a stretch to say that the construction of such a marvellous machine with such a low crash rate is negligent or an example of unacceptable quality; or (ii) refrain from imposing liability on the manufacturer of the vehicle responsible for the collision, even though this is probably—from a policy perspective—the best place for liability to be placed. As explained in *Todd's Law of Torts*[109]:

> The liability of a manufacturer for harm to third parties caused by its products need not be founded on negligence. Broad considerations of policy may favour a stricter regime.[110] As

---

109 Stephen Todd et al., *The Law of Torts in New Zealand*, 7th Edition (Thomson Reuters, 2016), 337–338.

110 G. Calabresi and J. T. Hirschoff (1972) 81 *Yale LJ* 1055: "Product Liability: Economic Analysis and the Law" (Symposium) (1970–1971), 38, *Univ of Chic L Rev*; United Kingdom Law Commission and Scottish Law Commission *Liability for Defective Products* (Law Com No 82 and Scot Law Com No 45, 1977); S. Waddams, *Products Liability*, 5th edition (Toronto:

between an innocent manufacturer and an innocent consumer it might be thought fairer that the risk of injury or loss should be borne by the former. After all, the manufacturer is in a position of overall control as regards the quality and safety of the product. Indeed, the manufacturer induces general consumer reliance simply by marketing the product and promoting its attributes. Arguably, considerations of deterrence and efficiency tend to point in the same direction. Thus the extra burden cast on the manufacturer by a rule of strict liability can operate as an incentive to take all possible care; the manufacturer is in a good position to insure against liability or build in the cost of compensation as part of the cost of the product; and it can be unnecessarily costly and inefficient for liability to be shifted along a chain of contracts before eventually it reaches the manufacturer.

This analysis pertains to the merits of strict liability versus negligence, but it is equally relevant to the merits of having liability in the Consumer Guarantees Act dependent on showing that a product is not of acceptable quality. And it seems particularly applicable to driverless vehicles. It would be far more efficient for manufacturers to cover the cost of the crashes for which their vehicles are responsible, build it into the cost of the vehicles, and thus spread that cost among all of their customers. If the superior safety claimed for these vehicles is to be believed, then this cost will be minimal. And those manufacturers that have greater success in building and designing safer vehicles will be able to charge less and gain a competitive advantage over their rivals.

It also seems desirable to avoid a situation where the courts—in order to engineer a socially desirable result whereby manufacturers are liable for all crashes caused by their vehicles—are tempted to conclude that manufacturers are negligent whenever their vehicles cause a crash. It does not

---

Craswell, 2011) at chapter 11; D.G. Owen, *Products Liability Law*, 2nd edition (St. Paul, MN: West Publishing, 2008).

seem fair to stigmatise manufacturers with the label of negligence if they have created a product that saves lives and performs better than anything that came before.

C. A New Product Liability Regime

For these reasons, I am recommending the statutory imposition of a product liability scheme on manufacturers for crashes that are caused by their vehicles while operating in a fully autonomous mode. There would be no requirement to show negligence on the part of the manufacturer, just that the crash had been caused by their vehicle. There is a risk that this could be perceived by manufacturers as an unfriendly legislative development to discourage the deployment of driverless vehicles. I hope that the preceding explanation shows that this is not the case. If the courts are likely to hold manufacturers responsible anyway, it is far better that this should be on the basis of a statutory product liability scheme than by branding them as negligent. And—as discussed earlier—many manufacturers are already confident enough in their product that they seem to be happy to assume this liability anyway.

There is no exact precedent in New Zealand for a statutory scheme setting out liability for civil damages from a product failure. The closest would be the Consumer Guarantees Act 1993, which allows damages to be obtained but only (i) by the owner of the product and (ii) where the product was not of acceptable quality. The scheme I am suggesting would be both narrower and broader than this. It would be narrower in that it only applies to one class of products—driverless vehicles—rather than all products. It would be broader in that there is no need to show that the product is not of acceptable quality, and damages would not be limited to the owner of the product. In some respects, it would be more similar to the statutory regime under the Maritime Transport Act 1994,[111] which requires the owner of a ship to pay the cost of cleaning up any pollution that escapes the ship (with limited defences).

---

111 See part 25 of the Maritime Transport Act 1994.

A product liability scheme for driverless vehicles will need to be clear about the circumstances under which a manufacturer will and will not be liable. I have suggested a new part 10A in the Land Transport Act 1998, with a new section 151A, as follows.

Part 10A

Liability for collisions involving driverless vehicles

151A Liability for collisions involving driverless vehicles

(1) This section applies where a person has suffered loss resulting from a collision caused by a vehicle in circumstances where, if an individual had been driving the vehicle, that individual would be liable for the loss and—

    (a) the cause of the collision was related to—

        (i)   the way the vehicle moved or failed to move;

        (ii) the way the vehicle was positioned;

        (iii) the failure of the vehicle to have its headlamps or tail lamps on in lighting conditions under which they should have been on;

        (iv) the failure of the vehicle to dip its headlamps; or

        (v)   the way that the vehicle signalled or failed to signal; and

    (b) the vehicle was driving itself at the time of the collision using an unsupervised autonomous mode of operation—

        (i)   within the circumstances under which the manufacturer has indicated the mode is capable of operating without supervision by an individual driver; or

        (ii) outside those circumstances and no individual who has operated the vehicle can be shown to be responsible for this.

(2) This section does not apply if any of the circumstances outlined in subsection (1)(a) were caused by inadequate maintenance or damage to the vehicle.

(3) Where this section applies any person who has suffered loss may obtain damages from the manufacturer of the vehicle.

This section would also rely on a new definition in section 2.

unsupervised autonomous mode of operation means a mode of operation of a vehicle in relation to which the manufacturer has indicated that, provided the vehicle is not directed to operate outside the circumstances under which the manufacturer has indicated the mode is capable of operating without supervision by an individual driver, no supervision by an individual is required.

Subsection (1) sets out the circumstances where the regime applies. There must be a person who has suffered loss resulting from a collision caused by a vehicle. That collision must have occurred in circumstances where, had an individual been driving, that individual would be liable for the loss. All the usual considerations as explored earlier in the section on liability with traditional vehicles will apply here. Did the vehicle fail to give way or signal? Did it fail to have its lights on at night?

Subparagraph (a) of subsection (1) then has a limited list of causes that must be involved before the regime can apply. This is because there are some causes for which it does not make sense to hold the manufacturer liable. For example, if an inadequately secured item falls off the vehicle and causes a collision, then this shouldn't be the manufacturer's responsibility. Nor should the manufacturer be responsible if a person in the vehicle was to yell out the window and distract a cyclist into crashing.

It does make sense to hold the manufacturer liable for collisions caused by the way the vehicle moves or fails to move. Likewise, if the vehicle is not moving but positioned in a place that causes a collision (e.g., stopped in the middle of the road around a blind corner), then the manufacturer should be held liable. The same applies if the vehicle was travelling in the dark without lights on, turning without signalling, or not dipping its headlamps and dazzling oncoming traffic.

However, if any of these circumstances was caused by inadequate maintenance or damage, then it does not make sense to hold the manufacturer liable. For example, if the bulbs/LEDs in the headlamps had been removed or disconnected, then the manufacturer shouldn't be blamed for that. Subsection (2) rules out the application of the liability regime in these circumstances. I recognize that there could be a countervailing view here in that perhaps the vehicles should be designed in a failsafe manner so that, for example, the vehicle would not operate in its autonomous mode at night unless the lights were working.

Subparagraph (b) of subsection (1) is a key provision. It sets out that the vehicle must—at the time of the collision—have been driving in an "unsupervised autonomous mode of operation." This is a defined term in section 2. It is important that the manufacturer should only be liable when the vehicle is in a truly driverless mode that was intended to be used by the manufacturer that way. When a manufacturer releases a mode that it intends to be used as a driverless mode, it will represent it as a mode that allows the vehicle to drive itself without supervision, but it will also have certain caveats that it is only capable of doing this in certain circumstances (for example, as explained earlier, in certain geographical areas that have been mapped and for which the vehicle has been tested and validated). Subsection (1)(b)(i) sets out that the vehicle must be driving itself within the "operational design domain" of the mode being used. I have described this as "the circumstances under which the manufacturer has indicated the mode is capable of operating without supervision by an individual driver." So if the vehicle had been directed by an individual to travel to a destination that necessarily took it outside of the geographical areas within which the manufacturer had indicated it was competent to operate, then the manufacturer should not be liable. As explored earlier, I recognize that there could be a countervailing view here; perhaps we should expect the manufacturer to ensure that their vehicle does not accept instructions that take it outside of its operational design domain. But, as discussed earlier, there may be circumstances where it is better that a vehicle should try to implement such instructions—for example, taking a person who has suffered a heart attack to the nearest hospital. People should be able to override the warning of the vehicle, but if they do, then the manufacturer should not be held responsible for any mishaps. The person who overrode the warning should be responsible; especially if they did so for a frivolous reason. Subsection (1)(b)(ii) sets out an exception to subsection (1)(b)(i). If the vehicle operated outside of its operational design domain despite receiving no instruction by a person to do this (perhaps it suffered some kind of malfunction), then the manufacturer should be responsible.

Finally, subsection (3) simply states that if all the foregoing conditions have been satisfied, then a person who has suffered loss as a result of the collision is able to recover damages from the manufacturer. This provision mirrors the language used in section 27(1) of the Consumer Guarantees Act 1993.

D. Recovery of Damages from Overseas Manufacturers

Most, if not all, of the manufacturers who might be liable under the proposed product liability regime will be overseas companies. Most are likely to have a presence in New Zealand, but some might not. It is possible that the presence in New Zealand of some smaller operators could be limited to the fact that someone has imported a few of their vehicles into the country.

This could pose some problems for a person seeking to recover damages, though I suspect in reality there will not be much difficulty.

In most cases, it would probably not be necessary for the courts to be involved. Most of these companies will be multinational companies with a reputation to protect. It would be sufficient for the claimant to submit a claim to the manufacturer, and if it is meritorious, the manufacturer will not resist it. At least they would not resist it for the sake of the minimal cost of property damage from a motor vehicle collision. The manufacturer will have access to all sorts of data and other information about the mode the vehicle was operating in, the instructions it received, the conditions of the road, the geographical location, and probably even video footage of the incident. It will be in an excellent position to judge the merits of the claim.

If the courts did have to become involved, then there are existing mechanisms to deal with this. The claim could be lodged in a New Zealand court, and if necessary, the claimant could commence an action in the company's home jurisdiction to enforce the New Zealand judgment. Alternatively, the claimant could pursue the company in its home jurisdiction from the outset. These options would be expensive and time-consuming, but as noted, they would be unlikely to be required in the vast majority of cases.

E. Software Updates

What if the owner of a vehicle neglects to accept over-the-air software updates for their vehicle, and this causes the vehicle to be involved in a collision? Should the manufacturer still be liable?

Ideally, this issue will not arise because the manufacturer would either ensure the updates occur automatically, or it would not allow the vehicle to operate in the relevant driverless mode unless and until the updates are accepted.

Alternatively, the manufacturer could allow the vehicle to be operated without updates but provide a warning to the operator that the vehicle is being operated outside of its operational design domain. If the operator chose to ignore this warning, then the operator would be liable for any collisions that resulted.

If the manufacturer allows the vehicle to be operated without updates and does not provide a warning that it is operating outside of its operational design domain, then the provisions described should operate to hold the manufacturer liable.

F. Duration of Liability

Vehicles can remain in service on the roads for many years. The average age of light passenger vehicles in 2014 was 14.3 years,[112] and there is no reason to assume that driverless vehicles will not stay on the roads for many years. Is it reasonable for the law to continue to hold manufacturers responsible for all this time?

---

112 http://www.ehinz.ac.nz/assets/Factsheets/Released-2015/EHI10-11-AverageAgeOfVehicleFleetInNZ2000-2014.pdf.

My view is that this will be related to the acceptable life span of the vehicle. Under the Consumer Guarantees Act 1993, the consumer has a right to expect a product to last a certain amount of time before breaking down or becoming obsolete. This varies depending on the product, and it is a reasonably subjective question. If a washing machine breaks down after three years, then it is not of acceptable quality and the consumer has a remedy. Electronic products like smartphones become obsolete after a certain amount of time when the manufacturer decides to discontinue the updates. The same will likely apply for driverless vehicles. After a certain period of time, it will be reasonable for the manufacturer of a driverless vehicle to cease providing software updates and other support. If this happens too early, then the consumer will have a remedy, just as if a washing machine broke down too early or the manufacturer stopped supporting their mobile phone too early. But, when it does happen, the manufacturer will be entitled to either (i) prevent the vehicle from operating in driverless mode or (ii) warn the operator that the vehicle will be operating outside of its operational design domain if operating in the driverless mode, and any liability for collisions can no longer accrue to the manufacturer.

G. Alternatives to a Product Liability Scheme

If the potential for driverless vehicles to substantially reduce collisions and the resulting damage and financial losses is as great as some hope, this would be a substantial benefit to society as a whole. It could be argued then that the responsibility for compensating losses on the rare occasions when driverless vehicles do cause damage should also be borne by society as a whole. Perhaps road users should contribute to a fund that provides no-fault compensation in the event that driverless vehicles cause damage.

There is a great deal of merit in this idea, but it is not workable at present. Who would contribute to this fund? Would it just be the owners of driverless vehicles? In that case, it would not be that different in practice to a product liability scheme. This is essentially what is happening with such a scheme, because manufacturers of driverless vehicles would build the cost of compensation into the cost of the vehicle or into the cost of software updates that would be needed to acquire new driverless modes.

Such a scheme might be worth considering if and when we get to the point that most roads are reserved for driverless vehicles.

Recommendation 5

Amend the Land Transport Act 1998 to insert new section 151A to create a statutory product liability regime for manufacturers of driverless vehicles in relation to crashes that are caused by their vehicles while operating in a fully autonomous mode.

Civil Liability for Personal Injury

A s discussed in chapter 6, the issue of liability is greatly simplified in New Zealand because there is no need to deal with liability for personal injury. Injuries that result from the operation of driverless vehicles will be compensated in exactly the same way as injuries that result from regular motor vehicles, under the universal no-fault accidental injury scheme administered by the Accident Compensation Corporation (ACC).

Compensation for these injuries is paid out of ACC's Motor Vehicle account, which is one of the five main accounts that are used to compensate people for personal injuries. The other accounts are the Work account (for work-related injuries), the Earners account (for non-work injuries by income earners), the Non-earners account (for non-work injuries by non-income earners), and the Treatment injury account (for injuries that result from medical treatment). As set out in section 213(2) of the Accident Compensation Act 2001, the Motor Vehicle account is funded from levies on petrol and through motor vehicle licence fees. The amount of these levies is set in the Accident Compensation (Motor Vehicle Account Levies) Regulations 2017. There are different levies depending on the model of the vehicle, the year it was manufactured, and whether it is petrol, non-petrol (e.g., diesel), or electric. Not all models are listed in the regulations, and there are generic levels for these vehicles. The levies are decided by the Minister of Transport after consultation in accordance with section 330 of the Accident Compensation Act. They are based on assessments of the safety of various vehicles. The levies for light passenger vehicles range from $17.38 up to $150.63. The first driverless vehicles will initially come under the generic classification and will pay the lowest rate of $17.68 (if petrol or electric) or $87.36 (if diesel). If they perform as safely as is hoped, it is possible that the Minister would eventually set even lower levies for driverless vehicles.

It is interesting to observe that the Motor Vehicle account receives no contributions from vehicle manufacturers. This means that motor vehicle manufacturers (of both driverless and non-driverless vehicles) are potentially receiving something of a subsidy in New Zealand. In other countries, such as the United States, if a manufacturing or design defect in a vehicle (for example defective brakes) causes a collision that results in a personal injury, the manufacturer might be liable to pay damages. In New Zealand, section 317 of the Accident Compensation Act 2001 bars proceedings for personal injury, so the manufacturer cannot be liable for damages. So the manufacturer is exempt from having to make any contribution to the cost of compensating for personal injury, even though their products could—in theory—be contributing to this cost.

This has not caused much concern over the years in relation to traditional cars, probably because there does not seem to be much of a problem with vehicle defects causing personal injuries. As noted in chapter 6, I was unable to find a single case in New Zealand of somebody making a claim for property damage resulting from a defective vehicle. It would also be very difficult to devise a method to collect levies from manufacturers. There is also a sense that New Zealand is thought to benefit from the vehicle safety assurance of other countries, such as the United States, without contributing to their cost, and so we shouldn't feel too aggrieved about this inadvertent potential subsidy.

If driverless vehicles do not perform as well as hoped when they are introduced and cause a lot of personal injuries, then there may be demand to revise this position. In the meantime, it seems prudent to wait and see if there is a problem. And if driverless vehicles perform poorly enough to cause a problem, then there may be a case to take regulatory action to remove problematic models from the road entirely, rather than letting them continue to cause personal injuries and trying to figure out a way to recover costs.

Overall then, I see no need to change any of the ACC legislation as it relates to driverless vehicles. It seems perfectly fit for purpose as it is.

8

Criminal Liability

There are hundreds of criminal offences that can be committed in connection with a motor vehicle in New Zealand. Some are serious, such as dangerous driving.[113] Where it causes death, dangerous driving can attract penalties of up to ten years' imprisonment, a $20,000 fine, and disqualification from driving.[114]

Other offences are less serious, such as failing to stop at a stop sign[115] or illegal parking.[116] While these lesser offences are still technically part of the criminal law, most people would not regard them as being truly "criminal."[117] Many of these less serious offences can be dealt with as

---

113 Driving or causing a motor vehicle to be driven at a speed or in a manner that, having regard to all the circumstances, is or might be dangerous to the public or to a person is an offence under section 35(1)(b) of the Land Transport Act 1998.

114 Section 36AA(2) Land Transport Act 1998.

115 Clause 4.1 of Land Transport (Road User) Rule 2004 stipulates that a driver approaching or entering a place where the vehicles moving in the direction in which the driver is travelling are controlled by a stop sign must stop his or her vehicle before entering the path of any possible vehicle flow at such a position as to be able to ascertain whether the way is clear for the driver to proceed. Failure to do this is classified as an offence by regulation 3(1) of the Land Transport (Offences and Penalties) Regulations 1999, which also sets the maximum penalty of $1,000.

116 Clause 6.4 of Land Transport (Road User) Rule 2004 prohibits a driver or person in charge of a vehicle from stopping, standing, or parking a vehicle on any part of a road contrary to the terms of a notice, traffic sign, or marking. Regulation 4(1) and schedule 1 of the Land Transport (Offences and Penalties) Regulations 1999 classify doing this as an infringement offence, with a variable scale of infringement fees set out in schedule 1B.

117 See page 11 of A. P. Simester and W. J. Brookbanks, *Principles of Criminal Law*, 4th edition (Thomson Brookers, 2012), which comments, "A parking offence, for example,

infringement offences,[118] which means the enforcement officer has the option of issuing an infringement notice[119] with an infringement fee instead of filing a charging document with a court. The least serious offences, such as illegal parking, can only be dealt with as infringement offences.[120]

A. What Will Be the Results of Applying Current Criminal Provisions to Vehicles with Driverless Technology?

The most advanced vehicles available to the public at the time of writing are not truly driverless in the sense of being able to operate without the supervision of a driver. They have not altered the legal landscape in terms of who is liable for various offences under different circumstances. The necessity for a supervising driver means they are really not much more than sophisticated versions of the kinds of cruise control and other driver assistance modes that drivers have been using for decades. The law treats the supervising drivers of these more sophisticated modes in the same way as the supervising driver of a vehicle using cruise control. A supervising driver is still the driver and is responsible in the same way.

The same cannot be said about the arrival of the first truly driverless vehicles. They will be represented by their manufacturers as being able to drive without a supervising driver or indeed without anyone in the vehicle at all. Our current criminal laws were not designed to deal with this. They

---

comprises an altogether different order of wrongdoing than murder. This is not to deny that traffic offences and their like are part of the criminal law, although perhaps they should not be. But most people in ordinary life distinguish minor, regulatory-type offences from 'true' crimes, and the element of public condemnation is and should be conveyed only by a conviction of the latter type."

118 For example, regulation 4(1) of the Land Transport (Offences and Penalties) Regulations 1999 classifies failing to stop at a stop sign as an infringement offence and sets the infringement fee at $150.

119 In accordance with sections 138 and 139 of the Land Transport Act 1998.

120 Clause 6.4 of Land Transport (Road User) Rule 2004 prohibits a driver or person in charge of a vehicle from stopping, standing, or parking a vehicle on any part of a road contrary to the terms of a notice, traffic sign, or marking. Regulation 4(1) and schedule 1 of the Land Transport (Offences and Penalties) Regulations 1999 classify doing this as an infringement offence, with a variable scale of infringement fees set out in schedule 1B.

rely on terms such as "driver" and—as a result—certain offences will not be able to be committed by driverless vehicles. For example, the provision that prohibits speeding[121] states that "a *driver* must not *drive* a vehicle at a speed exceeding the applicable speed limit" [emphasis added]. A vehicle without a driver can therefore break the speed limit without infringing this provision. The prohibition against transporting children without securing them properly [122] is also targeted at the "driver" and so will be similarly powerless to prevent the unsafe transportation of children.

Not all offence provisions are targeted solely at the "driver." There is a variety of expression in these provisions, which means it is something of a lottery as to which offences can and cannot be "committed" with a driverless vehicle and who the offender would be. The offence of dangerous driving[123] has—for reasons that are not entirely clear—been drafted in a wider manner than the speeding offence. It applies to a driver, but it also applies to someone who "causes a motor vehicle to be driven" in a dangerous way. It is therefore possible (though not certain) that the owner or operator could be considered to have caused the vehicle to be driven in a dangerous way and thus be guilty of the offence. The offence of careless driving,[124] which is less serious than dangerous driving, has been drafted in an even wider manner. It applies to anyone who "operates" a vehicle carelessly or without reasonable consideration, and "operates"[125] means to "drive or use the vehicle on a road, or to cause or permit the vehicle to be

121 Clause 5.1 of Land Transport (Road User) Rule 2004 prohibits speeding, and regulations 3 and 4 and schedule 1 of the Land Transport (Offences and Penalties) Regulations 1999 specify it as a regular offence and an infringement offence.

122 Clause 7.6 of Land Transport (Road User) Rule 2004 sets out the obligation for the driver to ensure passengers under seven use a child restraint, and regulations 3 and 4 of the Land Transport (Offences and Penalties) Regulations 1999 specify breach of this obligation as a regular offence and an infringement offence.

123 Driving or causing a motor vehicle to be driven at a speed or in a manner that, having regard to all the circumstances, is or might be dangerous to the public or to a person is an offence under section 35(1)(b) of the Land Transport Act 1998.

124 See section 37(1) of the Land Transport Act 1998, which sets out that the offence applies to any person who operates a vehicle carelessly or without reasonable consideration for other persons using the road.

125 See the definitions of "operate" and "operator" in section 2 of the Land Transport Act 1998.

on a road or to be driven on a road, whether or not the person is present with the vehicle." This could capture even more people, including people who are "using" the vehicle by riding in it. The same is true for reckless driving (an offence more serious than both careless and dangerous driving), which also applies to anyone who "operates" a vehicle recklessly.[126]

B. Is There a Better Way?

The haphazard and illogical distribution of liability described here is surely not desirable. It seems particularly problematic that the users of driverless vehicles could find themselves criminally liable for the actions of a vehicle over which they had no control (other than perhaps selecting the destination). It is unjust and it could discourage the uptake of driverless technology. But reforming this situation is easier said than done.

Whenever a vehicle does something—for example, speeding—that would have been an offence had a person been driving, we have three broad options in terms of liability.

Firstly, we could hold the user liable—although what is meant by the "user" is a difficult question in itself. Secondly, we could hold the manufacturer liable, in a similar way to the civil liability process set out in chapter 6.

Or thirdly, we could hold no one responsible, which would essentially be a decision to legalise the activity when performed by a driverless vehicle (because prohibiting something without a sanction is meaningless).

The Purpose of Criminal Law

In deciding which approach to take in relation to all the possible offences that might apply to driverless vehicles, it is useful to take a step back and remind ourselves why we have the criminal law at all. Why do we have certain activities or behaviours that have been criminalised as offences for which people can be penalised? What are these penalties designed to achieve?

---

126 Section 35(1)(a) of the Land Transport Act 1998.

Generally speaking, the criminalisation of certain behaviours is because they are thought to be immoral, harmful, or otherwise undesirable. In an ideal world, decisions about what is and is not an offence are made democratically, but even then, there can be problems if there is a majority that makes such decisions to the detriment of minorities.

Happily, the regulation of traffic in New Zealand has not been a particularly controversial area in this regard. Even though stakes are high when travelling in fast-moving metal boxes, ownership and use of vehicles is nearly universal, and everyone is a pedestrian, a passenger, or a motorist at some point. The biggest controversies are between people who use different modes of transport (for example, should cyclists be allowed to ride on the footpath?) and arguments about whether and how to encourage more environmentally and socially friendly modes of travel, such as public transport. Almost everyone agrees that actions like speeding or dangerous driving should be offences (even though they may sometimes object when the rules are applied to them personally and may disagree what speed limits should be and when and where they should apply).

The vast majority of the penalties imposed when somebody commits an offence on the road are minor fines. The more serious penalties include disqualification and—in the worst cases—imprisonment.

In the broader criminal arena, the main reason for imposing penalties and other orders is, of course, punishment. But punishment is not the sole objective. For example, when someone is sentenced to imprisonment for a serious offence, it is partly—at least in theory—a safety measure. If someone commits a murder, society is concerned they may do it again. Putting that person in prison with strict supervision is supposed to help to prevent this. In this regard, it is no more a punishment than the detention and quarantine that is legally imposed on people with a contagious disease for public health reasons.[127] Of course, people are often put in prison without a great deal of evidence that they pose a continuing

---

127 Sections 92I and 92ZA of the Health Act 1956 empowers the District Court to order the detention of individuals who pose a public health risk in a hospital or other suitable place.

danger to other people. Some murders or other violent crimes are one-off events, the result of an unlikely set of circumstances that are unlikely to arise again. And yet few would disagree that a murderer should go to prison, even if he or she poses no more danger than anyone else. Murder deserves punishment.

Other types of sentences can be pure safety measures, with no punitive aspect. Examples of these types of measures include orders barring sex offenders from specific locations, such as playgrounds, or forcing violent offenders to undergo activities that are designed to be rehabilitative.

And then there are the sentences that are purely for punishment. A monetary fine is usually regarded as less serious than imprisonment, but it performs no safety or other function, so it cannot be argued to serve any purpose other than punishment.

What is punishment for then? Why does the state deliberately inflict harm on individuals who have committed offences? At the risk of over-simplifying the long tradition of philosophical inquiry into this question, the two main theories are "consequentialist" and "non-consequentialist."

Consequentialist Justice

Consequentialists justify punishment on the grounds that it produces good consequences, usually by deterring future offending by the person being punished or other potential future offenders. It can also include the prevention of tit-for-tat blood feuds that would build up in bygone days when the administration of justice and punishment was left in the hands of the wronged party or that person's family and friends. If the state steps in to decide the punishment and impose it, there is far less scope for disproportionate retribution and an escalating series of retalia-tory measures.

There are different types of consequentalists. Utilitarians, like Jeremy Bentham, are consequentialists who believe that the greatest happi-ness of the greatest number is the foundation of morals and legislation. Bentham believed that "all punishment in itself is evil" and "it ought only to be admitted in as far as it promises to exclude some greater evil."[128] Consequentialism has its critics, such as those who fear that it is excessively pragmatic and could be used to justify overly severe punishment or even the punishment of innocents, if this could be shown to produce a net benefit by discouraging harmful behaviour.

Non-consequentialist or Retributive Justice

Non-consequentialists—or retributivists, as they are sometimes called— justify punishment on the basis that the offence is inherently morally wrong and those who are guilty of committing it deserve to be punished irrespective of whether this punishment has any other benefits. Retributivism has ancient roots, but it fell out of favour in the 1950s and 1960s as social workers, psychologists, and criminologists sought to use scientific methods and reform the penal system into an instrument to reduce offending. However those who hoped that it was about to become a medieval relic of the past were to be disappointed and retributivism made a comeback in the last quarter of the twentieth century, partly as a result of rising crime and disillusionment about the efficacy of using the penal system to reduce crime.

Applying Theories of Justice to Motor Vehicles

When it comes to the regulation of motor vehicles, it is possible to find both consequentialist and non-consequentialist/retributivist rationales for punishment. Most of the punishment dished out in the name of traffic regulation would probably be seen in purely consequentialist terms—it is necessary to discourage more risky behaviours such as speeding. But when a driver is responsible for serious harm or death then the punishment is more likely to be justified in retributivist terms.

We can now return to our earlier question about the three options for liability when a driverless vehicle commits an offence. When should we

---

128 Jeremy Bentham, *An Introduction to Morals and Legislation* (1789), Chapter XIII 1. II.

hold the user liable? Should the manufacturer ever be liable? Is it necessary to hold anyone liable?

Assigning Liability to the User of a Driverless Vehicle

There are many situations where it would make little sense to hold the user liable. The user may have been using the vehicle exactly as directed, and the extent of their control over the vehicle may be limited to simply selecting a destination. If that is the case then they have done nothing inherently morally wrong. There is no retributivist who would think that any kind of retributive punishment is warranted. As for consequentialist punishment, it is difficult to see how punishing a user under such circumstances could have any positive consequences. Given that the only choice the user made was whether or not to use a driverless vehicle, the only consequence of punishing such a user would be to discourage the use of driverless vehicles altogether.

But there are circumstances where it could make sense to impose penalties on a user, both for retributive and consequentialist reasons. What if the user directed the vehicle to operate in a way that the manufacturer specifically warned against (for example, operating it in a geographical area in which the manufacturer warned it was not capable of operating, due to lack of mapping information or conditions that the vehicle was not equipped to handle) and this resulted in the vehicle committing an offence? Or what if the offence was for something that was not within the control of the driverless vehicle, for example having an insecure load? Under these circumstances it could make sense to punish the user in order to discourage this kind of behaviour. And if the offending behaviour by the driver caused death or other serious harm then we would likely see retributivists clamouring for some Old Testament-style justice.

Assigning Liability to the Manufacturer of a Driverless Vehicle

As long as a manufacturer was acting in good faith and legitimately attempting to develop a safe vehicle, then it seems unlikely that even a staunch retributivist would call for retributive justice to be imposed for the actions of a driverless vehicle. It would surely take some sort of major corporate malfeasance whereby the manufacturer deliberately misrepresented the capability of a vehicle, in order to justify retributive punishment.

As for punishing manufacturers for consequentialist reasons, there are a number of arguments as to why the imposition of penalties on manufacturers might be ineffective and illogical as a way to encourage safety.

Firstly, even if these penalties were successful in encouraging manufacturers to try harder to produce vehicles that will always comply with speed limits and other restrictions, it could be argued that such compliant vehicles will not necessarily be any safer. If driverless vehicles are really going to be so superior to human-driven vehicles, then complying with speed limits and other restrictions may not be necessary for safety. It could even be argued that we do not need speed limits for driverless vehicles at all. The vehicle will take all the road conditions into account and drive at a speed that is safe for its skill level, and this could be faster than the speed limits that are set for human drivers. I do not think we should accept this line of reasoning, and I doubt it would ever be seriously advanced by manufacturers or other proponents of driverless vehicles (at least not in the early years). There may be scope for this kind of reasoning further down the line, if and when driverless vehicles prove their superiority, but not now.

A more compelling argument as to why fines might be ineffective is that manufacturers already have plenty of incentives to ensure that their vehicles obey the law and drive safely. If a driverless vehicle does not obey the law, then its manufacturer may face much bigger problems, such as consumer backlash and possible regulatory action (such as product recalls). And if fines are imposed in the same dollar amounts as those imposed on individuals, then they will be miniscule compared to these larger market and regulatory incentives.

Having No Liability for Offences Committed by Driverless Vehicles

As mentioned earlier, if we decide that there should be no liability for anyone when a driverless vehicle performs an action that would be an offence if there had been a driver, that is essentially a decision to legalise that action. Herein lies the basic reason why I think we need to impose liability. If we want driverless vehicles to be accepted then there needs to be some kind of recognition that they must play by the same rules as other vehicles.

This report is therefore recommending that penalties should be imposed on an appropriate party when a vehicle performs an action that would have been an offence if the vehicle were being driven by a person. The appropriate party will sometimes be the manufacturer, and it will sometimes be another party such as the user. Because manufacturers will invariably be corporate entities, it will be necessary that any penalties imposed on manufacturers are restricted to fines. The only other option would be to jail the employees or executives of manufacturers who would likely be based overseas. This would be fraught with difficulty and potential unfairness, and would risk scaring off manufacturers from New Zealand entirely.

For the sake of simplicity, I am proposing that—for the most part—fines for manufacturers should be the same fines that an individual would have received for driving the vehicle. But even this simple proposition is not simple to put into practice. How should we decide when a particular offence should be the responsibility of a manufacturer and not someone else?

C. Using Speeding as a Case Study

A useful entry point is to look more closely at the offence of speeding. Who should be held accountable if a driverless vehicle is detected speeding? To answer this question, we need to re-examine the different ways that driverless vehicles might be operated.

A driverless vehicle could be a personal vehicle that has an unsupervised autonomous highway driving mode. The operator has driven it to the highway and activated the highway mode with an instruction to drive itself a certain distance (perhaps to the desired off-ramp) and then notify the driver to take control. As driverless vehicles become more capable, then the vehicle would be able to operate autonomously not just on highways but on other roads as well. If the driverless vehicle was to make a mistake and travel too fast (perhaps by misreading a sign speed or due to an error in its database of what the speed limits are in different locations), then it seems logical that the manufacturer should be liable. A possible exception to this (as discussed in chapter 6) might be if the operator has instructed the vehicle to take a journey that necessarily takes it outside of its operational design domain.

Another likely way that a driverless vehicle might be being used at first would be as part of a ride-sharing taxi fleet. The vehicle could be a part of a fleet entirely made up of driverless vehicles (or a mixture of driverless vehicles and traditional human-driven Uber/Lyft vehicles), which is providing taxi services within a specific suburb via a ride-sharing app such as Uber or Lyft. These vehicles may not even have driver controls, and the "operator" would be nothing more than a passenger who has requested a ride using a ride-sharing app. Another variation on this could be something along the lines of the planned Tesla ride-sharing fleet, where personally owned Tesla vehicles can—with the push of a button—be sent into service in the fleet to earn money for the owner by providing ride-sharing services to people requesting rides via an app that manages the fleet. In these situations, safety and reliability may be being assured not just through the vehicle's internal systems but also through the ride-sharing app and other software that is ensuring that the vehicles stay within the geographical areas and other conditions that make up its operational design domain. If so, it may be more logical for the company that runs the ride-sharing app and software to be responsible for any mistake that leads to the vehicle speeding.

A possible legislative model for sorting through this quagmire of responsibilities is provided by the existing provisions in the Land Transport Act 1998 that address speeding by a regular (non-driverless) vehicle that has been detected by a speed camera. Before speed cameras were introduced, the only way of dealing with speeding vehicles was to have an enforcement officer with a radar gun who detected the speeding vehicle, gave chase, pulled over the vehicle, identified the driver, and issued an infringement notice to that driver. A speed camera is far more efficient in that it detects the speed of a vehicle automatically using radar and then automatically takes a photograph of the vehicle and its licence plate. The obvious problem is that there is no way the speed camera can know who was driving. Who has committed the offence? The law has solved this problem with section 133 of the Land Transport Act 1998.

133   Owner liability for moving vehicle offences and special vehicle lane offences

(1) Proceedings for a moving vehicle offence or a special vehicle lane offence may be taken against 1 or more of the following persons:

    (a) the person who allegedly committed the offence:

    (b) the person who, at the time of the alleged offence, was registered under Part 17 in respect of the vehicle involved in the offence (or, if the offence is alleged to have been committed before the commencement of section 242, a person who, at the time of the alleged offence, was registered as the owner, or one of the owners, of that vehicle in a register kept under section 18 of the Transport (Vehicle and Driver Registration and Licensing) Act 1986):

    (c) a person who, at the time of the alleged offence, was lawfully entitled to possession of the vehicle involved in the offence (whether jointly with any other person or not);—

whether or not (in the case of a person referred to in paragraph (b) or paragraph (c)) the person is an individual or was the driver or person in charge of the vehicle at the time the alleged offence was committed.

(2) In proceedings taken against a person under paragraph (b) or paragraph (c) of subsection (1), in the absence of proof to the contrary, it must be presumed that—

    (a) the defendant was the driver or person in charge of the vehicle at the time of the alleged offence (whether or not the person is an individual); and

(b) the acts or omissions of the driver or person in charge of the vehicle at that time were the acts or omissions of the defendant.

(3) It is a defence to proceedings against a person for a moving vehicle offence or a special vehicle lane offence if another person has, by virtue of an order under the Criminal Procedure Act 2011 or the Summary Proceedings Act 1957, become liable to pay a fine or costs, or both, in respect of the offence.

(4) It is a defence to proceedings against a person under paragraph (b) or paragraph (c) of subsection (1) if,—

    (a) at the time the alleged offence was committed,—

        (i) the person was not lawfully entitled to possession of the vehicle (either jointly with any other person or severally); or

        (ii) another person was driving the vehicle; and

    (b) immediately after becoming aware of the alleged offence, the person advised the enforcement authority in writing that, at the time the offence was committed, he or she was not lawfully entitled to possession of the vehicle or another person was driving the vehicle (as the case may be); and

    (c) the person has given the enforcement authority a statutory declaration—

        (i) identifying the driver, by giving—

            (A) the full name and full address of the driver; and

            (B) any other identifying particulars, so far as they are within the person's knowledge, such as the driver's date of birth, occupation, telephone number; or

        (ii) establishing that the person could not identify the driver, after taking all reasonable steps to do so.

(5) In proceedings for a moving vehicle offence or a special vehicle lane offence, a statutory declaration given under subsection (4) is, in the absence of proof to the contrary, sufficient evidence of the matters stated in the declaration; and it is admissible for all purposes of any proceedings under this section.

As the title indicates, this section deals with moving vehicle offences[129] and special vehicle lane offences.[130] Speeding offences come under the definition of "moving vehicle offence." An important element of this definition is that the offence needs to have been detected by "approved vehicle surveillance equipment" (i.e., a speed camera).

Subsection (1)(b) allows proceedings to be taken against the registered owner of the vehicle that has been photographed speeding (or committing another of the eligible offences). In the absence of evidence to the contrary, the owner is presumed—for the purposes of enforcement proceedings—to be the driver (see subsection (2)). This applies even if the owner is not an individual (i.e., it is a company).

The first step for an enforcement authority after the offence has been detected is to initiate proceedings against the registered owner. If the owner was not driving the vehicle at the time, then that owner has the option of defending the offence using once of the two defences in subsection (4)(a).

The first of these defences is that the owner was not lawfully entitled to possession of the vehicle at the time of the offence (for example, the owner is a rental car company, and the vehicle was rented out at the time of the offence). The owner can establish this defence by providing legal documentation (for example a rental agreement) showing that someone else was entitled to possession. The owner is also required to take reasonable steps to identify the driver and, if successful, make a statutory

---

129 See definition in section 2 of the Land Transport Act 1998. "A *moving vehicle offence* means an offence detected by approved vehicle surveillance equipment that is—(a) a speeding offence; or (b) an offence in respect of the failure to comply with the directions given by a traffic signal or a traffic sign that is a variable traffic or lane control sign; or (c) any offence against regulations made under this Act or the Transport (Vehicle and Driver Registration and Licensing) Act 1986 that is declared by regulations under this Act to be a moving vehicle offence for the purposes of this definition; or (d) a toll offence."

130 There is no definition of "special vehicle lane offence" (which may be an accidental omission in the legislation). But there is a definition of "special vehicle lane" in section 2 of the Land Transport Act 1998, which cross refers to a definition in clause 1.6 of the Land Transport (Road User) Rule 2004. This definition makes it clear that the offence is intended to refer to a situation where a vehicle is detected in a bus lane or other special lane in which it is not authorised to travel.

declaration identifying that driver. If the owner does these things, then the defence has been made out and will stand unless rebutted by further evidence. This also provides the enforcement agency with sufficient evidence to bring proceedings (under subsection (1)(a)) against the possessor of the vehicle.

The second of these defences is that someone else was driving the vehicle. This can be used by an owner or possessor of a vehicle, and it can also be established without any evidence other than a statutory declaration identifying the driver. If the alleged driver disputes that he or she was in fact driving, then that driver can bring evidence to the contrary. A court will then have to weigh up that evidence against any further evidence brought by the owner/possessor and decide who is telling the truth and who is lying or mistaken.

This section works efficiently. When speed cameras were first being considered, one might have been forgiven for thinking that the potential difficulties with evidence and proving who was actually driving the vehicle might make them unworkable in practice. But section 133 shows how a system can be designed that can, in most cases, function fairly without the need for anything more than quite minimal evidence. The default imposition of liability on the owner and the possessor produces the necessary incentive for those parties to divulge who the responsible party is (if it is someone different to the owner or possessor). And its use of statutory declarations means that it is not onerous for an owner or possessor to shift the liability onto the person with whom it rightfully belongs. In the majority of cases, the alleged driver really is the driver, knows he or she is in the wrong, and does not dispute the liability. The need for further evidence is limited to those less common cases where someone (the owner or the possessor or the alleged driver) decides to lie or is mistaken about who was driving. The one potential problem with section 133 is that when a person is implicated as the liable driver by a statutory declaration, then section 133(5) requires that he or she *prove* that he or she is not the driver to escape liability. This seems a little unfair and potentially unjust. An alleged driver might be falsely accused and have had nothing to do with the offence, but the burden is on that person to produce some sort of conclusive rebuttal evidence, or he or she will be liable on the basis of someone else's declaration.

D. Adapting the Speed Camera Provisions in the Land Transport Act to Deal with Speeding by Driverless Vehicles

The approach used in section 133 can be adapted to create a mechanism to appropriately allocate liability when driverless vehicles are caught speeding by a speed camera.

The first issue to address is the fact that driverless vehicles can perform some actions that would be illegal if there was a human driver (such as speeding and others) without breaking the law. Of course a speed camera will not be able tell the difference between a human-driven and a driverless vehicle. It will still take a photo of a speeding driverless vehicle, and an infringement notice will be sent to the owner in accordance with section 133(1)(b). But if the owner knows that the vehicle was driving itself at the time it was speeding, he or she will be able to get out of the ticket by producing evidence (perhaps vehicle operation logs) that there was no one driving the vehicle. With no driver, there is no "speeding offence," which means no "moving vehicle offence" and therefore no ability to take proceedings against the owner under section 133(1). If the owner had rented the vehicle out, then the owner could transfer liability to the possessor in the usual way, and the possessor could get out of the ticket in the same way. Or if the owner or possessor had lent the vehicle to a friend or employee, then the owner could transfer liability to that person who—again—could get out the ticket by showing there was no driver and hence no offence. If the vehicle has no steering wheel or other controls, then this is conclusive evidence in itself that the vehicle must have had no driver.

I propose that this can be addressed by creating a new category of offence called a "driverless vehicle offence." This would be done by inserting two new definitions in section 2 of the Land Transport Act 1998.

driverless vehicle means a vehicle that is travelling on a road at a time when there is no individual driving it

driverless vehicle offence means an offence that is committed when a driverless vehicle moves or fails to move, signals or fails to signal, fails to use or dip its headlamps, or carries passengers in a way that would constitute an offence against this Act or rules, regulations or bylaws made under this Act, if an individual had been driving the vehicle.

These new definitions are intended to ensure that if an owner or possessor produces evidence showing that the vehicle was driving itself, this does not completely preclude the operation of section 133 as it previously did. The definition of "driverless vehicle" is simply a vehicle that is travelling on a road at a time when no individual is driving it. The definition of "driverless vehicle offence" then incorporates this definition to set out that a driverless vehicle offence is committed whenever a driverless vehicle performs certain actions that would constitute an offence had the vehicle been driven by an individual person. So when an owner or possessor produces evidence showing that their speeding vehicle was driving itself, that person is qualifying the vehicle as a "driverless vehicle" and establishing that a "driverless vehicle offence" has been committed because the vehicle "move[d]...in a way that would constitute an offence...if an individual had been driving the vehicle." This, in turn, means that a "speeding offence"[131] has been committed. And a speeding offence—when detected by a speed camera—qualifies as a "moving vehicle offence,"[132] which brings section 133(1) into play and allows proceedings to be taken against the owner or possessor.

The new definitions do not do the whole job however. There are still gaps. If an owner or possessor had lent the vehicle to someone, it would

---

131 Defined in section 2 of the Land Transport Act 1998 as an offence that consists solely of exceeding a speed limit.
132 Defined in section 2 of the Land Transport Act 1998 as including a speeding offence.

be preferable if that owner or possessor still had the option of using the defence in section 133(4)(a)(ii) that someone else was driving the vehicle and unfair if he or she didn't have that option. But the owner or possessor may have difficulty doing so because—in the case of a vehicle with a driverless mode—it may not be accurate to say that the person he or she lent it to had been "driving" it. And in the case of a driverless vehicle without driver controls, it would be impossible for someone else to have been driving it.

Where an owner or possessor has not lent the vehicle out and was using it him- or herself, the potential unfairness goes in the other direction. We may have fixed the issue with driverless vehicles not being able to commit a speeding offence, but the owner or possessor will still be able to get out of the offence every time because of the way that subsection (2) in section 133 has been drafted. Subsection (2) allows proceedings to be taken against that person as if he or she were the driver, but only "in the absence of proof to the contrary." So the owner or possessor could— again—provide evidence that the vehicle was driving itself, rebutting the presumption in section 133(2) that he or she was the driver. This would preclude any possibility of liability, even though there are circumstances (as described in the following) where the person probably should be liable.

Therefore, in order to make section 133 work for driverless vehicles, some amendments to that section and another new definition in section 2 are necessary. An amended version of section 133 is set out here.

133   Owner liability for moving vehicle offences and special vehicle lane offences

(1) Proceedings for a moving vehicle offence or a special vehicle lane offence may be taken against 1 or more of the following persons:

  (a) the person who allegedly committed the offence <u>or who was allegedly using the vehicle at the time of the offence</u>:

  (b) the person who, at the time of the alleged offence, was registered under Part 17 in respect of the vehicle involved in the offence (or, if the offence is alleged to have been committed before the commencement of section 242, a person who, at the time of the alleged offence, was registered as the owner, or one of the owners, of that vehicle in a register kept under section 18 of the Transport (Vehicle and Driver Registration and Licensing) Act 1986):

(c) a person who, at the time of the alleged offence, was lawfully entitled to possession of the vehicle involved in the offence (whether jointly with any other person or not);—

whether or not (in the case of a person referred to in paragraph (b) or paragraph (c)) the person is an individual or was the driver or <u>user</u> <u>or</u> person in charge of the vehicle at the time the alleged offence was committed.

(2) In proceedings taken against a person under ~~paragraph (b) or paragraph (c) of~~ subsection (1)~~, in the absence of proof to the contrary,~~ it must<u>, unless the defendant has a defence under subsections (3) or (4),</u> be presumed that—

(a) the defendant was the driver or person in charge of the vehicle at the time of the alleged offence (whether or not the person is an individual); and

(b) the acts or omissions of the driver or person in charge of the vehicle <u>or of the vehicle itself</u> at that time were the acts or omissions of the defendant.

(3) It is a defence to proceedings against a person for a moving vehicle offence or a special vehicle lane offence if another person has, by virtue of an order under the Criminal Procedure Act 2011 or the Summary Proceedings Act 1957, become liable to pay a fine or costs, or both, in respect of the offence.

(4) It is a defence to proceedings against a person under ~~paragraph (b) or paragraph (c) of~~ subsection (1) if,—

(a) at the time the alleged offence was committed,—

(i) <u>in respect of proceedings under paragraph (b) or paragraph</u> <u>(c) of subsection (1),</u> the person was not lawfully entitled to possession of the vehicle (either jointly with any other person or severally); or

(ii) <u>in respect of proceedings under paragraph (b) or paragraph (c) of subsection (1),</u> another person was driving <u>or using</u> the vehicle; <u>or</u>

(iii) <u>the vehicle was driving itself using an unsupervised autonomous mode of operation within the circumstances under which the manufacturer has indicated the mode is capable of operating without supervision by an individual driver, or outside those circumstances and the person is not responsible for this;</u> and

(b) immediately after becoming aware of the alleged offence, the person advised the enforcement authority in writing that, at the time the offence was committed, <u>one of the defences in subsection (4) (a) applied and identified which one</u> ~~he or she was not lawfully entitled to possession of the vehicle or another person was driving the vehicle (as the case may be)~~; and

(c) <u>if using the defence under subsection (4)(a)(i) or (ii),</u> the person has given the enforcement authority a statutory declaration—

(i) identifying the driver <u>or user</u>, by giving—

(A) the full name and full address of the driver <u>or user</u>; and

(B) any other identifying particulars, so far as they are within the person's knowledge, such as the driver <u>or user</u>'s date of birth, occupation, telephone number; or

(ii) establishing that the person could not identify the driver <u>or user</u>, after taking all reasonable steps to do so; and

(d) <u>if using the defence under subsection (4)(a)(iii), the person has given the enforcement authority a statutory declaration establishing that, at the time the alleged offence was committed, the vehicle was driving itself using an unsupervised mode of operation in either of the circumstances described in that subsection.</u>

(5) In proceedings for a moving vehicle offence or a special vehicle lane offence, a statutory declaration given under subsection (4) is, in the absence of ~~proof~~ <u>evidence</u> to the contrary, sufficient evidence of the

matters stated in the declaration; and it is admissible for all purposes of any proceedings under this section <u>and section 151B</u>.

The new definition in section 2 is as follows.

unsupervised autonomous mode of operation means a mode of operation of a vehicle in relation to which the manufacturer has indicated that, provided the vehicle is not directed to operate outside the circumstances under which the manufacturer has indicated the mode is capable of operating without supervision by an individual driver, no supervision by an individual is required.

The first thing to note is that the defence in section 133(4)(a)(ii) has been expanded so that the owner/possessor does not necessarily have to allege that someone was "driving" the vehicle. He or she can instead state that someone else was "using" it. This is particularly important in the case of a vehicle that literally cannot be driven because it has no driver controls.

The next thing to note is the removal of the words "in the absence of proof to the contrary" from section 133(2). As explained earlier, leaving these words in would allow an owner/possessor/user of a speeding driverless vehicle to completely evade liability by showing evidence that the vehicle was driving itself and rebutting the presumption that he or she was the "driver." Removing these words stops that. We cannot *just* remove these words and do nothing else, however, because this would mean that the owner/possessor/user is *always* going to be responsible when his or her driverless vehicle is detected speeding by a speed camera, even though all the person might have done was instruct the vehicle to drive from point A to point B and it was the vehicle's "fault" that the speed limit was exceeded. We need to replace these words so that they can still avoid liability where the vehicle was being used properly in a "driverless" mode. This is what I have done with a cross-reference in section 133(2) to the defences listed in subsection (4)(a). We then need to add a new defence to subsection (4)(a), which applies when the vehicle is in a driverless mode under appropriate circumstances. This defence appears as new subparagraph (iii) and has the following elements. Firstly, the vehicle must have been "driving itself using an unsupervised autonomous mode of operation." The term "unsupervised autonomous mode of operation" is one of the new definitions in section 2 and is intended to capture any truly driverless mode that the manufacturer has indicated is capable of operating without supervision (as long it is not directed to operate outside of its operational design domain). Secondly, the vehicle must not have actually been directed to operate outside of its operational design domain. This is logical because people should not expect to be able to avail themselves of the "driverless vehicle defence" if they were not using the vehicle in accordance with the manufacturer's instructions. Subsection (4)(d) then provides that the owner must make a statutory declaration about the circumstances that are claimed to enable use of the defence. Subsection (5) then allows this declaration to be sufficient evidence of this on its own, unless there is evidence to the contrary.[133]

If the owner was not the possessor of the vehicle at the time of the offence (for example, if the owner is a rental car company and the customer was in possession), then section 133 operates as before, with subsection (4)(a)(i) of that section, allowing the owner to escape liability and pass it to that customer/possessor. That possessor is then able to use the driverless vehicle defence in the same way as an owner. Alternatively, if the owner or possessor had lent the vehicle to someone (a friend or employee), then he or she can use the defence in section 133(4)(a)(ii) and transfer the liability to that person.

---

133 I have changed "proof to the contrary" to "evidence to the contrary" for the reason already discussed. Subsection (5) also applies to a person who has been implicated on the strength of a statutory declaration with no other evidence, and it seems harsh that such a person should have the burden to *prove* his or her innocence.

All of this only does half the job though. It ensures that owners/possessors/users are not unjustly fined for speeding or other offences committed by driverless vehicles detected by cameras, while still being held accountable when they are responsible. But it does not ensure that the appropriate person is held responsible (such as the manufacturer, in the appropriate circumstances). It also does nothing when the offence was not detected by a camera.

To achieve this, I propose a new section 151B to be inserted into a new part 10B in the Land Transport Act 1998.

Part 10B

Driverless vehicle offences and driverless vehicle parking offences

151B   Driverless vehicle offences

(1) Proceedings for a driverless vehicle offence that is not a restraint or seat belt offence may be taken against any 1 or more of the following persons—

    (a) the manufacturer of the vehicle, if the vehicle was driving itself at the time of the alleged offence using an unsupervised autonomous mode of operation:

        (i) within the circumstances under which the manufacturer has indicated the mode is capable of operating without supervision by an individual driver;

        (ii) outside those circumstances, and no individual who has operated the vehicle can be shown to be responsible for this;

    (b) the person who, at the time of the alleged offence, was registered under Part 17 in respect of the vehicle involved in the offence; or

    (c) a person who, at the time of the alleged offence, was lawfully entitled to possession of the vehicle involved in the offence (whether jointly with any other person or not);

    (d) a person who activated the mode that the vehicle was using to drive itself at the time of the alleged offence;-

whether or not the person is an individual or was the driver or user or person in charge of the vehicle at the time the alleged offence was committed.

(2) Proceedings for a driverless vehicle offence that is a restraint or seat belt offence may be taken against any 1 or more of the following persons—

    (a) if there was no person aged 16 years or over in the vehicle at the time of the alleged offence, the person who, at the time of the alleged offence, was registered under Part 17 in respect of the vehicle involved in the offence;

    (b) if there was no person aged 16 years or older in the vehicle at the time of the alleged offence, a person who, at the time of the alleged offence, was lawfully entitled to possession of the vehicle involved in the offence (whether jointly with any other person or not;

    (c) if there was no person aged 16 years or older in the vehicle at the time of the alleged offence, a person who was responsible for the presence in the vehicle of the passenger to whom the restraint or seat belt offence relates;

    (d) any person aged 16 years or older in the vehicle at the time of the alleged offence (as if that person were the driver)

(3) Proceedings taken against a person under subsections (1) or (2) will, unless the defendant has a defence under subsections (4), (5) or (6) proceed as if—

    (a) the defendant were the driver of the vehicle at the time of the alleged offence (whether or not the person is an individual); and

    (b) the events that constitute the driverless vehicle offence at the time of the alleged offence were the acts of omission of the defendant.

(4) It is a defence to proceedings against a person for a driverless vehicle offence if another person has, by virtue of an order under the Criminal Procedure Act 2011 or the Summary Proceedings Act 1957, become liable to pay a fine or costs, or both, in respect of the offence .

(5) It is a defence to proceedings against a person under paragraph (b), (c) or (d) of subsection (1) if,—

  (a) at the time the alleged offence was committed,—

    (i) the person was not lawfully entitled to possession of the vehicle (either jointly with any other person or severally);

    (ii) the mode that the vehicle was operating in was not activated by the person; or

    (iii) the vehicle was driving itself using an unsupervised autonomous mode of operation within the circumstances under which the manufacturer has indicated the mode is capable of operating without supervision by an individual driver, or outside those circumstances and the person is not responsible for this; and

  (b) immediately after becoming aware of the alleged offence, the person advised the enforcement authority in writing that, at the time the offence was committed, one of the defences in paragraph (a) applied and identified which one; and

  (c) the person has given the enforcement authority a statutory declaration—

    (i) identifying a person who was lawfully entitled to possession of the vehicle (if relying on the defence in subsection (a)(i)), by giving—

      (A) the full name and full address of that person; and

      (B) any other identifying particulars, so far as they are within the person's knowledge, such as the driver's date of birth, occupation, or telephone number;

    (ii) establishing that, at the time the alleged office was committed, the mode that the vehicle was operating in was not activated by the person and—

      (A) identifying the person who did activate the mode by giving their full name and address and any other identifying particulars, so far as they are within the person's knowledge, such as date of birth, occupation telephone number; or

(B) establishing that the person could not identify the person who activated the mode, after taking all reasonable steps to do so; or

(iii) establishing that, at the time the alleged offence was committed, the vehicle was driving itself using an unsupervised mode of operation in either of the circumstances described in subparagraph (a)(ii) (if relying on the defence in that subparagraph);

(6) It is a defence to proceedings against a person under subsections (2)(a) and (2)(b) if,—

(a) at the time the alleged offence was committed, —

(i) the person was not lawfully entitled to possession of the vehicle (either jointly with another person or severally); or

(ii) another person was responsible for the presence in the vehicle of the passenger to whom the restraint or seat belt offence relates ;

(b) immediately after becoming aware of the alleged offence, the person advised the enforcement authority in writing that, at the time the offence was committed, the defence in paragraph (a) applied and identified which one; and

(c) the person has given the enforcement authority a statutory declaration identifying a person who was lawfully entitled to possession or the person who was responsible for the presence in the vehicle of the passenger to whom the restraint or seat belt offence relates, by giving—

(i) the full name and address of that person; and

(ii) any other identifying particulars, so far as they are within the person's knowledge, such as the person's date of birth, occupation or telephone number.

(7) In proceedings for a driverless vehicle offence, a statutory declaration given under subsections (5) or (6) or section 133(4) is, in the absence of evidence to the contrary, sufficient evidence of the matters stated in the declaration; and it is admissible for all purposes of any proceedings under this section.

(8) In proceedings for any offence involving a vehicle:

(a) the defendant may make a statutory declaration establishing that, at the time the alleged offence was committed, the vehicle was driving itself using an unsupervised mode of operation in either of the circumstances described in subsection (5) (a) iii);

(b) in the absence of evidence to the contrary, that declaration is sufficient evidence of the matters stated in the declaration; and it is admissible for all purposes of any proceedings under this section; and

(9) Where a driverless vehicle offence has been committed, no proceedings may be taken for any other type of offence that may arise from the events that constitute the driverless vehicle offence.[134]

In the case of a speeding offence (or other moving vehicle offence or a special vehicle lane offence) detected by a camera, a successful use of the "driverless vehicle defence" means that a driverless vehicle offence has been committed as set out in the definition in section 2. The amendment to section 133(5) allows the statutory declaration that facilitated the defence to be sufficient evidence of a driverless vehicle offence for the purposes of section 151B.

The enforcement agency will now put on hold the proceedings against the initial defendant (who has utilised the driverless vehicle defence) and commence proceedings against the manufacturer of the vehicle under

---

134 This is intended to ensure that if someone directs the vehicle to drive from A to B and the vehicle commits an offence, that person is not prosecuted under the regular offence provision, for example "causing a motor vehicle to be driven in a dangerous way", or "operating" the vehicle. If someone is to be prosecuted, it must be through this provision to make sure they have the opportunity to shift the blame to the manufacturer where appropriate.

section 151B(1)(a). The manufacturer is then able to analyse the vehicle's data, assess whether the initial defendant's statutory declaration was correct, and, if it is not, produce evidence to rebut that declaration.

There are a number of ways in which the declaration might not be correct. It may be that the vehicle was not driving in an unsupervised autonomous mode of operation and—in fact—was not even in a semiautonomous mode (such as a supervised highway driving mode). This would probably mean that the initial defendant had to have been actively driving the car and is probably trying to get out of the ticket by lying about the car driving itself. Regardless of the initial defendant's motives, evidence from the manufacturer that the declaration was incorrect and the vehicle was not even in a semiautonomous mode will overturn the presumption made by section 151B(7) that the declaration is sufficient evidence to allow the initial defendant to utilise the defence in section 151B(5)(a)(iii). So the initial defendant's defence collapses, but, more fundamentally, the overturning of the presumption that the vehicle was driving itself means that it was not a "driverless vehicle", there was no "driverless vehicle offence" and section 151B does not apply at all. Proceedings can then be recommenced as a normal speed camera offence against the initial defendant under section 133(a), (b) or (c), depending on whether that initial defendant was the user, owner or possessor of the vehicle. Another possibility is that the vehicle was driving itself, but it was in a supervised semiautonomous mode (not an unsupervised autonomous mode of operation, and perhaps the initial defendant's declaration that it was is an honest mistake). In that case, the vehicle was still a "driverless vehicle" at the relevant time and the offence is still a "driverless vehicle offence", but the statutory declaration that makes out the grounds for the manufacturer's liability under section 151B(1)(a) and underpins the initial defendant's defence under section 151B(5)(a)(iii) has been overturned. Liability for the speeding offence therefore reverts back to the initial defendant, and proceedings can be recommenced against him or her under section 151B(1) (b), (c) or (d), again depending on whether that initial defendant was the owner, possessor or user. A further possibility is that the vehicle was in an unsupervised autonomous mode of operation, but it was not operating within the circumstances under which the manufacturer has indicated the mode is capable of operating without supervision by an individual driver (for example, it might have been outside of the geographical area the vehicle is capable of operating within). If so, then the manufacturer needs to establish whether the vehicle strayed outside of these circumstances itself or whether this was due to a direction from the person operating the vehicle. If the latter, then the grounds for the manufacturer's liability under section 151B(1)(a) have not been made out and the initial defendant is liable under section 151B(1)(b), (c) or (d). If the former, then the grounds for the manufacturer's liability have been made out and the manufacturer is liable under section 151B(1)(a).

In the case of an offence that is not detected by a camera, there will be no statutory declaration, but section 151B will still be engaged if there is direct evidence from an enforcement officer of a driverless vehicle offence. This direct evidence could arise in a number of ways.

When any vehicle is observed by an enforcement officer to be speeding or driving dangerously (or doing anything else that constitutes an offence), then the officer will usually give chase, draw up behind the vehicle, and signal it to stop using lights, sirens or both. If that vehicle is using a driverless mode, then events could unfold in a number of different ways.

If the driverless vehicle has the capacity to recognise these signals, it will pull over. The officer will walk up to the vehicle and look inside. The vehicle may have no occupants at all, in which case there is direct evidence that the offence that was committed was a driverless vehicle offence. The enforcement agency will bring proceedings against the owner under section 151B(1)(b). The owner may then use one of the defences in section 151B(5)(a) if they are available. The owner might be able to show that he or she was not entitled to possession (section 151B(5)((a)(i)) and shift liability on to the possessor. Or the owner (or the possessor if liability has been shifted to them) might be able to use the defence in section 151B(5)(a)(ii) that they did not activate the driverless mode and shift the liability to the person who did (the user). Then whoever is left holding the liability (owner,

possessor or user) would be able to use the defence in section 151B(5)(a)
(iii) by making a statutory declaration that the vehicle was driving itself,
using an unsupervised autonomous mode of operation.

Or the vehicle may have occupants but no steering wheel or other
driver controls, which would also constitute direct evidence of a driverless
vehicle offence. If there are occupants and driver controls, then the officer
has no evidence (yet) that a driverless vehicle offence has been committed (even if none of the occupants are sitting in the driver's seat; this is not
conclusive because the person in that seat could have moved while the
officer was walking up). At first, the officer will likely assume that the person in the driver's seat was driving and proceed accordingly. Or if there is
no one in the driver's seat, the officer will enquire as to who was driving. In
either case, the occupant or occupants will inform the officer that no one
was driving; the vehicle was driving itself. The officer would be wise at this
point to collect the names and details of any occupants (in case the claim
that the vehicle was driving itself falls down later), but, for now, this would
also constitute direct evidence of a driverless vehicle offence.

It is possible that the officer would not believe the claim that the
vehicle was driving itself (especially in the early days of driverless vehicles being used) and would commence proceedings for a regular speeding offence against the person the officer thought was the driver. The
defendant in those proceedings is then able to make a statutory declaration under section 151B(8)(a) that the vehicle was driving itself, using an
unsupervised mode of operation either (i) within the circumstances under
which the manufacturer has indicated the mode is capable of operating
without supervision by an individual driver or (ii) outside those circumstances and the defendant is not responsible for this. This then means
that—under section 151B(8)(b)—the statutory declaration is sufficient evidence that a driverless vehicle offence has been committed. And under
section 151B(9) any further proceedings must be for a "driverless vehicle
offence." The enforcement authority could then still bring proceedings
against the defendant under section 151B(1)(d) as the person who activated the autonomous mode. But this would be a fairly pointless exercise

because the defendant would immediately reissue the statutory declaration under section 151B(5)(c)(iii) and activate the defence provided by section 151B(5)(a)(iii). So the enforcement authority would instead commence proceedings against the manufacturer under section 151B(1)(a). We then have a replay of the scenario described earlier where the manufacturer can produce evidence to rebut the defendant's defence (in which case proceedings will recommence against the defendant under section 151B(1)(d), or the manufacturer will have to accept liability under section 151B(1)(a).

If the officer was inclined to believe the claim that the vehicle was driving itself, that officer would still require a statutory declaration to provide the evidence needed to proceed against the manufacturer (and could use the threat of regular speeding proceedings against the person making the claim as an incentive for him or her to produce the declaration).

If the driverless vehicle does not have the capacity to recognise flashing lights as a signal to pull over, then either (i) one of the occupants might be able to manually pull the vehicle over or (ii) there may be no occupants or the occupants may not be able to pull it over for whatever reason (perhaps they are asleep, perhaps there are no driver controls, perhaps they do not want to pull over). In that case, the officer will likely do what an officer normally does when a vehicle does not stop: pull in front of the vehicle and bring it to a halt on the side of the road. If there are occupants in the vehicle, then we are back to the scenario described earlier when the occupants will claim to the officer that the vehicle was driving itself, and the same sequence of events will occur. If there are no occupants (or at least no adult occupants), then proceedings will be commenced against the owner under section 151B(1)(b). The owner may then use one of the defences in section 151B(5)(a) if they are available. The owner might be able to show that he or she was not entitled to possession (section 151B(5)((a)(1)) and shift liability on to the possessor. Or the owner (or the possessor if liability has been shifted to the possessor) might be able to use the defence in section 151B(5)(a)(ii) that he or she did not activate the driverless mode and shift the liability to the person who did (the user). Then whoever is left holding the liability (owner, possessor or user) would be able to use the defence in section 151B(5)(a)(iii) by making a statutory declaration that the vehicle was driving itself using an unsupervised autonomous mode of operation. We are then back to the scenario where the manufacturer is able to produce evidence rebutting this, or it must accept liability.

E. Other Driverless Vehicle Offences

The provisions I have proposed have been described with reference to speeding offences, but they are designed to capture other offences too.

The full definition of "driverless vehicle offence" has been framed to capture a range of offences that are appropriate to be treated as driverless vehicle offences, while also excluding inappropriate offences. This definition is repeated here for easy reference.

driverless vehicle offence means an offence that is committed when a driverless vehicle moves or fails to move, signals or fails to signal, fails to use or dip its headlamps, or carries passengers in a way that would constitute an offence against this Act or rules, regulations or bylaws made under this Act, if an individual had been driving the vehicle.

A large number of offences will be captured on the basis that they are something that would result when a driverless vehicle "moves or fails to move in a way that would constitute an offence…if an individual had been driving the vehicle."

The offence of dangerous driving[135] would be captured on this basis. Just like speeding, it can be committed by the driver. Unlike speeding, it can also be committed by someone who "causes a motor vehicle to be

---

135 Driving or causing a motor vehicle to be driven at a speed or in a manner that, having regard to all the circumstances, is or might be dangerous to the public or to a person is an offence under section 35(1)(b) of the Land Transport Act 1998.

driven" in a dangerous way. This means it is possible that an enforcement agency might seek to bring proceedings against a person who directed a vehicle to undertake a journey. If so, the provisions should still operate to ensure that liability ends up with the appropriate party. The defendant would be able to make a declaration under section 151B(8) that the vehicle was driving itself, and section 151B(9) will require the enforcement agency to bring any proceedings as a driverless vehicle offence under section 151B. Everything would then proceed in the same way as a speeding offence, with liability able to fall on a range of persons (including the manufacturer) depending on the circumstances.

The offences of careless driving[136] and reckless driving[137] would also be captured on the same basis. Both are phrased so as to apply to any person who "operates" a vehicle carelessly or recklessly. The word *operates* is defined[138] very widely to include driving a vehicle, but also using it and causing or permitting it to be on the road or driven on the road whether or not he or she is present with the vehicle. This opens up the possibility for enforcement authorities to go after a wide range of people who might be connected in some way with the driverless vehicle. But, as with dangerous driving, any defendant is able to make a declaration under section 151B(8) and require the enforcement agency to bring any proceedings as a driverless vehicle offence under section 151B.

The offence of failing or refusing to comply with a signal or request by an enforcement officer to stop a vehicle[139] is another offence that would be captured by "moves or fails to move." As explored earlier, driverless

---

136 See section 37(1) of the Land Transport Act 1998, which sets out that the offence applies to any person who operates a vehicle carelessly or without reasonable consideration for other persons using the road.

137 Section 35(1)(a) of the Land Transport Act 1998.

138 See the definitions of "operate" and "operator" in section 2 of the Land Transport Act 1998.

139 Enforcement officers have a power under section 114 of the Land Transport Act 1998 to signal or request the driver of a vehicle to stop the vehicle as soon as practicable. And under section 52(1)(c) of that Act, a person who fails or refuses to comply commits an offence.

vehicles may or may not have the capacity to recognize flashing lights and pull over. If they do not, then it might be desirable to have a prosecution policy not to prosecute driverless vehicles for failing to stop or even a statutory exemption (at least at first). This would mean relying on officers pulling in front of them to stop them. This would be undesirable if they were having to do it frequently, so this is something that could be revisited if driverless vehicles were not living up to expectations in this regard.

Other offences will not necessarily be captured by the "moves or fails to move" terminology. For example, the offence of failing to signal an intention to move to the left or right[140] is only indirectly related to the vehicle's movement. But it would still be captured by the definition of "driverless vehicle offence" because it is an example of where a vehicle "signals or fails to signal...in a way that would constitute an offence...if an individual had been driving the vehicle." As with speeding, it can only be committed by a driver, so everything would proceed in the same manner as a speeding offence. The other signalling offences are also captured in the same manner.

The offence of failing to use headlamps during the hours of darkness[141] would be captured as a driverless vehicle offence because it is an example where a vehicle "fails to use...its headlamps...in a way that would constitute an offence...if an individual had been driving the vehicle." Similarly, the offence of failing to dip headlamps for another driver[142] would be captured because the vehicle "fails to...dip its headlamps." These offences

---

140 Clauses 3.10(3) and (3) of the Land Transport (Road User) Rule 2004 require a driver to signal the intention to move left or right, and regulations 3 and 4 of the Land Transport (Offences and Penalties) Regulations 1999 specify failure to do this as a regular and an infringement offence.

141 Clause 8.3(3) of the Land Transport (Road User) Rule 2004 requires a driver to use headlamps after the hours of darkness, and regulations 3 and 4 of the Land Transport (Offences and Penalties) Regulations 1999 specify failure to do this as a regular and an infringement offence.

142 Clause 8.3(2)(a) of the Land Transport (Road User) Rule 2004 requires a driver to dip the vehicle's headlamps whenever they would be likely to interfere adversely with the vision of another driver on the road. Regulations 3 and 4 Land Transport (Offences and Penalties) Regulations 1999 specify this as a regular and an infringement offence.

are also committed by a driver, so everything proceeds as with a speeding offence.

There are a range of offences for which it would not make sense for the manufacturer to be liable under any circumstances.

For example, the offence of not keeping a vehicle in an appropriate condition[143] is committed by the "operator" of the vehicle and so potentially applies to a wide range of people. A manufacturer should not be responsible for the condition in which their vehicles are kept, and there is no need for this offence to be treated any differently when the vehicle involved is a driverless vehicle. The definition of "driverless vehicle offence" is therefore designed not to capture this offence, because it does not directly relate to the way a vehicle "moves or fails to move, signals or fails to signal, fails to use or dip its headlamps, or carries passengers." Similar considerations apply for the offence of operating a vehicle on a road without displaying a warrant of fitness.[144]

Another category of offence that can be left alone is the offences involving excess breath alcohol.[145] These apply only to a person driving or attempting to drive a motor vehicle. Persons who are merely riding in a driverless vehicle cannot commit this offence under current law, and this is how it should be. They are merely passengers. One of the main advantages of driverless vehicles is that people who might be tempted to drive drunk would use a driverless mode instead.

The offence of failing to report an accident involving injury or death[146] presents an interesting dilemma. At first glance, it seems technically feasible for a driverless vehicle to have the capability of knowing when it has

---

143 Clause 8.9 of Land Transport (Road User) Rule 2004 requires the operator to keep the vehicle in an appropriate condition, and regulations 3 and 4 and schedule 1 of the Land Transport (Offences and Penalties) Regulations 1999 specify a breach as a regular offence and an infringement offence.

144 See section 34(1)(b) of the Land Transport Act 1998.

145 Section 56 Land Transport Act 1998.

146 Section 22(3) of the Land Transport Act 1998 sets out the obligation to report, and section 47(2) of that Act specifies that it is an offence to fail to do this without reasonable excuse.

been involved in a collision and to comply with this reporting requirement by simply reporting all collisions (perhaps by sending an e-mail to the police with time and place and other details). It may be that manufacturers would build this functionality into their vehicles regardless of whether there is a legal requirement. On the other hand this might prove more difficult than it appears, so, on balance, I think it would be better not to require this from manufacturers (in case doing so presents too much of a deterrent to manufacturers releasing their vehicles in New Zealand). The definition of "driverless vehicle offence" has therefore been drafted with the intention of not capturing this offence. The offence will still apply to any riders in the vehicle (unless they have a reasonable excuse, such as being asleep) so they would be expected to phone the police if their vehicle was involved in a serious collision. Similar considerations apply for the offence of failing to stop and ascertain whether a person has been injured following an accident arising from the operation of a vehicle.[147] It is reasonable to expect riders in a driverless vehicle to manually stop the vehicle after an accident (if they can) and check if everyone is OK.

Offences relating to the inadequate restraint of children (for example failing to ensure passengers under the age of seven years use a child restraint[148]) present something of a special case. These are offences that can only be committed by a "driver," and this therefore results—under current law—in there being no requirement for children in driverless vehicles to be adequately restrained. If we want the same restraint requirements to apply in driverless vehicles (and surely we do if children are to be kept safe), then we need these offences to be captured by the definition of "driverless vehicle offence." At the same time, it would make no sense for manufacturers to ever be liable for these types of restraint offences. I propose that this can be dealt with as follows. Firstly, the definition of

---

147 Section 22(1) of the Land Transport Act 1998 sets out the obligation to stop and ascertain injury, and section 35(1) of that Act specifies that it is an offence to fail to do this without reasonable excuse.

148 See clause 7.6 of the Land Transport (Road User) Rule 2004 and regulations 3 and 4 of the Land Transport (Offences and Penalties) Regulations 1999.

"driverless vehicle offence" as proposed for section 2 does capture these offences. If a child was found to be inadequately restrained in a driverless vehicle, then this would be an example where a driverless vehicle "carries passengers in a way that would constitute an offence...if an individual had been driving the vehicle." Secondly, the proposed new section 151B contains subsection (2), which is designed to allocate liability for these offences. It utilises a new definition for a "restraint and seat belt offence" to be inserted in section 2 of the Land Transport Act 1998.

restraint or seat belt offence means any offence resulting from the breach of a requirement to ensure that a person is properly restrained by an approved child restraint or a seat belt.[149]

Subsection (2) sets out a range of people who can be liable for the offence. Firstly, if there is anyone in the vehicle aged sixteen or over, then he or she would be liable under section 151B(2)(d). That person is essentially in the position of the driver in terms of being responsible for ensuring that children in the vehicle are properly restrained. There is no defence.[150] If there is no one in the vehicle aged sixteen or over, then there may be a case for the offence of leaving a child without reasonable supervision and care,[151] but it would also open up other potential defendants for liability under the other subparagraphs of subsection (2). The enforcement authority would initially commence proceedings against the owner under section 151B(2)(a). The owner will be liable unless he or she can make a statutory

---

149 Note, another option would be to cross refer to the offences of breaching clauses 7.6, 7.7, 7.8 and 7.9 of the Land Transport (Road User) Rule 2004, but then this reference would need to be updated if the rules changed.

150 There may be a practical problem with this provision in cases where a child and his or her parent/guardian/minder are riding in a shared vehicle along with unrelated co-passengers who just happen to be sharing the same vehicle. If the parent/guardian/minder of the child failed to restrain the child, then the co-passengers would be equally liable along with the negligent parent/guardian/minder. Any unfairness here could potentially be addressed via a prosecution policy that ensured enforcement action in such cases is restricted to the parent/guardian/minder.

151 Section 10B of the Summary Offences Act 1981.

declaration under section 151B(6)(c) so as to use one of the defences in section 151B(6)(a). The first defence in section 151B(6)(a)(i) is the same defence that owners can use for the other offences, namely that they were not entitled to possession of the vehicle (perhaps they are a rental car company). If successful, this defence would make that possessor potentially liable under section 151B(2)(b). The second defence in section 151B(6)(a)(ii) that can be used by the owner or the possessor is that another person was responsible for the presence of the child in the vehicle. He or she would essentially be saying that even though it was "his or her vehicle," someone else was using it and put the child in it. That person would then become responsible under section 151B(2)(c), unless he or she can produce evidence to rebut the statutory declaration.

F. Parking Offences

As discussed in chapter 3, driverless vehicles will at some stage have the ability to drive off and park themselves. This raises the possibility that they may park illegally.

Illegal parking is the offence of stopping, standing, or parking a vehicle on any part of a road contrary to the terms of a notice, traffic sign, or marking.[152] It applies to a driver, but due to the fact that—even with a normal human-driven vehicle—there will not necessarily be a driver at the time a parking offence is committed (for example if the vehicle was left parked beyond the time limit), the offence provisions have been drafted so as to also apply to a "person in charge of a vehicle."

The detection of an illegally parked vehicle by an enforcement officer has a lot in common with the detection of a speeding vehicle by a speed camera. There is usually no opportunity for the officer to question a driver or other person in charge of the vehicle. It is not surprising then that the Land

---

152 Clause 6.4 of Land Transport (Road User) Rule 2004 prohibits a driver or person in charge of a vehicle from stopping, standing, or parking a vehicle on any part of a road contrary to the terms of a notice, traffic sign, or marking. Regulation 4(1) and schedule 1 of the Land Transport (Offences and Penalties) Regulations 1999 classifies doing this as an infringement offence.

Transport Act 1998 has—in the form of section 133A—a provision that attributes liability in the first instance to the owner of the vehicle, using a similar approach to that used by section 133 for speed camera offences.

133A   Owner liability for stationary vehicle offences

(1) Proceedings for a stationary vehicle offence may be taken against 1 or more of the following persons (whether or not, in the case of a person referred to in paragraph (b) or (c), the person is an individual or was the driver, person in charge, or user of the vehicle at the time the alleged offence was committed):

(a) the person who allegedly committed the offence:

(b) The person who, at the time of the alleged offence, —

    (i) was registered as the owner, or one of the owners, of the vehicle involved in the offence in a register kept under section 18 of the Transport (Vehicle and Driver Registration and Licensing) Act 1986; or

    (ii) was the registered person in respect of the vehicle under Part 17 of the Act:

(c) the person who, at the time of the alleged offence, was lawfully entitled to possession of the vehicle in the offence (whether or not jointly with any other person).

(2) Subject to subsection (4), in any proceedings taken against a person under subsection (1)(b) or (c), in the absence of proof to the contrary, it must be presumed that—

(a) the person was the driver, person in charge, and user of the vehicle at the time of the alleged offence (whether or not the person is an individual); and

(b) the acts or omissions of the driver, person in charge, or user of the vehicle at that time were the acts or omissions of the first-mentioned person.

(3) It is a defence to proceedings taken against a person for a stationary vehicle offence if the person proves that another person has, by virtue

of an order under the Criminal Procedure Act 2011 or the Summary Proceedings Act 1957, become liable to pay a fine or costs, or both, in respect of the offence.

(4) It is a defence to proceedings taken against a person under subsection (1)(b) or (c) if—

   (a) the person proves that, at the time the alleged offence was committed,—

     (i) he or she was not lawfully entitled to possession of the vehicle (either jointly with any other person or individually); or

     (ii) another person was unlawfully in charge of the vehicle; and

   (b) as soon as practicable after becoming aware of the alleged offence, he or she advised the enforcement authority in writing that, at the time the offence was committed, he or she was not lawfully entitled to possession of the vehicle or another person unlawfully had charge of the vehicle, as the case may be; and

   (c) he or she has given the enforcement authority a statutory declaration that—

     (i) identifies another person who was, at the time of the alleged offence, lawfully entitled to possession, or was unlawfully in charge, of the vehicle by providing—

       (A) the full name and full address of the other person; and

       (B) any other identifying particulars that are known to the person making the declaration (for example, the other person's date of birth, occupation, and telephone number); or

     (ii) establishes that the person making the declaration was unable to identify the other person after taking all reasonable steps to do so.

(5) In the case of any stationary vehicle defence, any defence available under subsection (3) or (4) is in addition to and not in substitution for any defences available under the enactment creating the offence.

This section applies to all "stationary vehicle offences" which are defined[153] as including parking on a road contrary to any Act, regulation or bylaw. This allows proceedings to be taken against the owner of an illegally parked vehicle under section 133A(1)(b). For the purposes of those proceedings, the owner will, under section 133A(2), be presumed to be the "driver, person in charge and user" of the vehicle at the time of the offence. If the owner was not in possession of the vehicle (e.g., it was rented out or stolen), he or she may make a statutory declaration under section 133A(4)(c) and use the defence in section 133A(4)(a). Proceedings can then be taken against the possessor under section 133A(1)(c).

If a driverless vehicle were to park itself illegally, then the owner or possessor would be liable as described earlier. While that owner would have the opportunity to try to dispute this liability by producing evidence that the vehicle parked itself and that this constituted proof to defeat the presumption in section 133A(2) that they should be treated as the "driver, person in charge, or user," it is difficult to predict how the courts would view such an attempt. They would probably consider that the owner/possessor was still the "person in charge or user" of the vehicle (particularly if he or she was the person who was in the vehicle last and who directed it to go and park itself).

As a matter of policy, it would seem desirable if there was less uncertainty about when a person can be said to be a person in control and liable for a parking offence. And it would be desirable if there was potential for the manufacturer to be liable in circumstances where their product is at fault.

This could be achieved using a similar approach to that used here for speeding and other offences. This would involve amendments to section 133A as follows.

---

153 The definition of "stationary vehicle offence in section 2 of the Land Transport Act 1998 consists of parking in any portion of a road, in breach of any Act, regulation or bylaw. It also includes other offences specified as such in regulations, and four have been set out in schedule 7 of the Land Transport (Offences and Penalties) Regulations 1999."

133A   Owner liability for stationary vehicle offences

(1) Proceedings for a stationary vehicle offence may be taken against 1 or more of the following persons (whether or not, in the case of a person referred to in paragraph (b) or (c), the person is an individual or was the driver, person in charge, or user of the vehicle at the time the alleged offence was committed):

(a) the person who allegedly committed the offence:

(b) The person who, at the time of the alleged offence, —

    (i) was registered as the owner, or one of the owners, of the vehicle involved in the offence in a register kept under section 18 of the Transport (Vehicle and Driver Registration and Licensing) Act 1986; or

    (ii) was the registered person in respect of the vehicle under Part 17 of the Act:

(c) the person who, at the time of the alleged offence, was lawfully entitled to possession of the vehicle in the offence (whether or not jointly with any other person).

(2) ~~Subject to subsection (4), i~~ In any proceedings taken against a person under subsection (1)(b) or (c), ~~in the absence of proof to the contrary,~~ it must <u>unless the defendant has a defence under subsections (3), (4) or (4A),</u> be presumed that—

(a) the person was the driver, person in charge, and user of the vehicle at the time of the alleged offence (whether or not the person is an individual); and

(b) the acts or omissions of the driver, person in charge, or user of the vehicle at that time were the acts or omissions of the first-mentioned person.

(3) It is a defence to proceedings taken against a person for a stationary vehicle offence if ~~the person proves that~~ another person has, by virtue of an order under the Criminal Procedure Act 2011 or the Summary Proceedings Act 1957, become liable to pay a fine or costs, or both, in respect of the offence.

(4) It is a defence to proceedings taken against a person under subsection
(1)(b) or (c) if—
  (a) ~~the person proves that,~~ at the time the alleged offence was
    committed,—
    (i) he or she was not lawfully entitled to possession of the vehicle
      (either jointly with any other person or individually); or
    (ii) another person was unlawfully in charge of the vehicle; and
  (b) as soon as practicable after becoming aware of the alleged offence,
    he or she advised the enforcement authority in writing that, at the
    time the offence was committed, he or she was not lawfully enti-
    tled to possession of the vehicle or another person unlawfully had
    charge of the vehicle, as the case may be; and
  (c) he or she has given the enforcement authority a statutory declara-
    tion that—
    (i) identifies another person who was, at the time of the alleged
      offence, lawfully entitled to possession, or was unlawfully in
      charge, of the vehicle by providing—
      (A) the full name and full address of the other person; and
      (B) any other identifying particulars that are known to the
         person making the declaration (for example, the other
         person's date of birth, occupation, and telephone num-
         ber); or
    (ii) establishes that the person making the declaration was unable
      to identify the other person after taking all reasonable steps to
      do so.

<u>(4A) It is a defence to proceedings taken against a person under subsection</u>
<u> (1)(b) or (c) for a parking offence if—</u>
<u> (a) at the time the alleged offence was committed, the vehicle was</u>
<u>   parked in a position—</u>
<u>   (i) that had been selected by the vehicle using an unsupervised</u>
<u>   autonomous mode of operation that the manufacturer has</u>
<u>   indicated is capable of operating without committing a parking</u>
<u>   offence; or</u>

> (ii) that resulted from a failure by the vehicle, while using an unsu-
> pervised autonomous mode of operation that the manufacturer
> indicated was capable of executing a direction to park in a spe-
> cific position, to execute a direction from the person to park in
> a specific position that was available at the relevant time; and

> (b) the mode of operation was operating within the circumstances
> under which the manufacturer has indicated the mode is capable
> of operating without supervision by an individual driver, or outside
> those circumstances and the person is not responsible for this; and

> (c) as soon as practicable after becoming aware of the alleged offence,
> he or she advised the enforcement authority in writing that, at the
> time the offence was committed, one of the defences in subsection
> (4)(a) applied and identified which one; and

> (d) he or she has given the enforcement authority a statutory decla-
> ration establishing that, at the time the alleged offence was com-
> mitted, the vehicle was parked in a position as described in either
> subsection (4)(a)(i) or (ii).

(5) In the case of any stationary vehicle defence, any defence available
under subsections (3), or (4) or (4A) is in addition to and not in substitution for any defences available under the enactment creating the
offence.

(6) In proceedings for a stationary vehicle offence, a statutory declaration
given under subsections (4) or (4A) is, in the absence of proof to the
contrary, sufficient evidence of the matters stated in the declaration;
and is admissible for all purposes of any proceedings under this section,
and section 151C.

The first thing to note about the amended section 133A is that the owner
or possessor may no longer merely use "proof to the contrary" to rebut
the presumption in subsection (2) that he or she was the "driver, person
in charge, and user of the vehicle." He or she must instead use one of
the existing defences (as explained earlier) or a new "driverless vehicle"
defence that has been added at subsection (4A). As discussed earlier, it

would be difficult anyway for an owner or possessor to use the fact that a car had "parked itself" to get out of the offence. These amendments preserve the ability of the owner or possessor of an illegally parked driverless vehicle to avoid liability but only in appropriate circumstances. And those circumstances will be where the vehicle had been instructed to go and find parking under circumstances where it was reasonable to believe that the vehicle would be able to find a legal park. For example, the manufacturer may offer a parking mode where the user can "save" a parking location, such as a home garage, in the vehicle's memory, and the vehicle can be instructed to navigate to that location and safely park there. Or the manufacturer may offer a more advanced mode whereby the user does not have to specify a location and the manufacturer has indicated the vehicle is capable of finding its own park in the vicinity. It may seem difficult to imagine how a manufacturer could offer such a mode. How can the manufacturer guarantee that the vehicle would find a park without knowing if there are any available parks nearby? It may not turn out to be possible, but the point is that if a manufacturer does figure out a way to do it (perhaps by partnering with specialised parking buildings that allow a driverless vehicle to electronically "check" if there is a free park and to reserve and pay for it before accepting the parking instruction from its user), then the law should cater for this possibility. And the user should not be penalised if he or she relies on the mode and it makes a mistake and parks illegally.

The practical effect of these changes would be as follows. A rider is taking a journey in a driverless vehicle. It reaches its destination, and the user gets out and instructs the vehicle to go and park. It might be a direction to park in a specific location, or it might be an instruction to find a park within a certain radius. Whatever the direction is, it is something that the manufacturer had indicated was within the capabilities of the vehicle.

Later the vehicle is found by an enforcement officer to be illegally parked. Perhaps it is parked on yellow lines. Perhaps it parked in a five-minute zone and stayed there too long. Perhaps it parked too close to a driveway. It is possible that enforcement officer may have witnessed the vehicle parking by itself. It is more likely the officer will have come across the vehicle later and will not know whether it was parked by a human driver or not. In either case, the officer will treat it as he or she would any other parking offence and commence proceedings against the owner under section 133A(1)(b). The owner then has the option of deploying one of the defences set out in subsections (4) or (4A). Subsection (4) is the existing defence that he or she was not lawfully entitled to possession when the alleged offence was committed (in which case that lawful possessor can become liable under section 133A(1)(c)) or that the vehicle was stolen (in which case the thief, if identified, will be liable under section 133A(1)(a)). Subsection (4A) is the new "driverless vehicle" defence. This applies if the vehicle was parked in a position that had been selected by the vehicle using an "unsupervised autonomous mode of operation"[154] that the manufacturer had indicated is capable of operating without committing a "parking offence."[155] So if the manufacturer had indicated that the vehicle was capable of executing a direction to "go and find a legal park" and the vehicle parked itself illegally, then this defence is available. The other way the defence can be used is if the illegal position that the vehicle was parked in resulted from a failure by the vehicle, while using an unsupervised autonomous mode of operation that the manufacturer indicated was capable of executing a direction to park in a specific position, to execute a direction to park in that position (provided that position was available at the relevant time). This defence is available if the user was utilising a mode that the manufacturer indicated allowed the vehicle to be directed to go and park in a specific location, and it failed to do this and parked itself illegally. The important caveat to this defence is that it only applies if the preselected park was actually available. If the vehicle arrives to find the park occupied or blocked and so has to go and find somewhere else, which turns out to be illegal, then the user is responsible. The

---

154 As defined in section 2.
155 Also defined in section 2.

rationale here is that if the user is going to use this mode, it is his or her responsibility to ensure that the preselected park is going to be available.

Both of these defences are subject to the additional caveat (in section 133A(4A)(b)) that the mode of operation must not be operating outside of the circumstances within which the manufacturer indicated it was capable of performing, or if it was, this must have been due to a mistake whereby the vehicle itself accidentally strayed outside of these circumstances.

The defendant (who may be the owner or the possessor) can issue a statutory declaration about this under subsection (6), and this then provides sufficient evidence to make out the defence.

We then need a provision that can allocate the liability for the offence through to the manufacturer if this is justified or return it back to the human defendant if it is not. This is what the new section 151C, together with a new definition for "driverless vehicle parking offence" is intended to do.

151C   Driverless vehicle parking offences

(1) Proceedings for a driverless vehicle parking offence may be taken against 1 or more of the following persons :

   (a) the manufacturer of the vehicle if—

      (i) at the time the alleged offence was committed, the vehicle was parked in a position—

         (A) that had been selected by the vehicle using an unsupervised autonomous mode of operation that the manufacturer has indicated is capable of operating without committing a parking offence; or

         (B) that resulted from a failure by the vehicle, while using an unsupervised autonomous mode of operation that the manufacturer indicated was capable of executing a direction to park in a specific position, to execute a direction to park in a specific position that was available at the relevant time; and

(ii) the mode of operation was operating within the circumstances under which the manufacturer has indicated the mode is capable of operating without supervision by an individual driver, or outside those circumstances and the person is not responsible for this.

(b) The person who, at the time of the alleged offence, —

(i) was registered as the owner, or one of the owners, of the vehicle involved in the offence in a register kept under section 18 of the Transport (Vehicle and Driver Registration and Licensing) Act 1986; or

(ii) was the registered person in respect of the vehicle under Part 17 of the Act:

(c) the person who, at the time of the alleged offence, was lawfully entitled to possession of the vehicle in the offence (whether or not jointly with any other person).

(2) Proceedings taken against a person under paragraph (b) or paragraph (c) of subsection (1)) will, unless the defendant has a defence under subsections (4) or (5), proceed as if—

(a) The defendant were the driver, person in charge and user of the vehicle at the time of the alleged offence (whether or not the person is an individual); and

(b) The events that constitute the driverless vehicle parking offence at the time of the alleged offence were the acts or omissions of the defendant.

(3) It is a defence to proceedings against a person for a driverless vehicle offence if another person has, by virtue of an order under the Criminal Procedure Act 2011 or the Summary Proceedings Act 1957, become liable to pay a fine or costs, or both, in respect of the offence.

(4) It is a defence to proceedings against a person under paragraph (b) or (c) of subsection (1) if,—

(a) at the time the alleged offence was committed,—

(i) The person was not lawfully entitled to possession of the vehicle (either jointly with any other person or severally); or

(ii) another person was unlawfully in charge of the vehicle; and

(b) immediately after becoming aware of the alleged offence, he or she advised the enforcement authority in writing that, at the time the offence was committed, he or she was not lawfully entitled to possession of the vehicle or another person unlawfully had charge of the vehicle, as the case may be; and

(c) the person has given the enforcement authority a statutory declaration that—

　(i) identifies another person who was, at the time of the alleged offence, lawfully entitled to possession, or was unlawfully in charge, of the vehicle by providing—

　　(A) the full name and full address of the other person; and

　　(B) any other identifying particulars that are known to the person making the declaration (for example, the other person's date of birth, occupation, and telephone number); or

　(ii) establishes that the person making the declaration was unable to identify the other person after taking all reasonable steps to do so.

(5) It is a defence to proceedings taken against a person under paragraph (b) or (c) of subsection (1) if—

(a) at the time the alleged offence was committed, the vehicle was parked in a position—

　(i) that had been selected by the vehicle using an unsupervised autonomous mode of operation that the manufacturer has indicated is capable of operating without committing a parking offence; or

　(ii) that resulted from a failure by the vehicle, while using an unsupervised autonomous mode of operation that the manufacturer indicated was capable of executing a direction to park in a specific position, to execute a direction from the person to park in a specific position that was available at the relevant time; and

(b) the mode of operation was operating within the circumstances under which the manufacturer has indicated the mode is capable of operating without supervision by an individual driver, or out-side those circumstances and the person is not responsible for this; and

(c) as soon as practicable after becoming aware of the alleged offence, he or she advised the enforcement authority in writing that, at the time the offence was committed, one of the defences in paragraph (a) applied and identified which one; and

(d) he or she has given the enforcement authority a statutory decla-ration establishing that, at the time the alleged offence was com-mitted, the vehicle was parked in a position as described in either subsection (4)(a)(i) or (ii).

(6) In proceedings for a driverless vehicle parking offence, a statutory dec-laration given under subsections (4) or (5) or section 133(4A) is, in the absence of evidence to the contrary, sufficient evidence of the matters stated in the declaration; and is admissible for all purposes of any pro-ceedings under this section.

(7) Where a driverless vehicle parking offence has been committed, no proceedings may be taken for any other type of offence that may arise from the events that constitute the driverless vehicle offence.[156]

The new definition (in section 2) would be as follows.

driverless vehicle parking offence means an offence that is committed when: (i) a vehicle is found parked in a way that would constitute an offence against this Act or rules, regulations or bylaws made under this Act, if an individual had been driving the vehicle; and (ii) the vehicle was a driverless vehicle while it was being parked.

---

156 this is intended to ensure that if someone directs the vehicle to go and park and the vehicle commits an offence, that person is not prosecuted under the regular offence provi-sion, for example "being in charge of the vehicle" when it parked illegally. If someone is to be prosecuted, it must be through this provision to make sure they have the opportunity to shift the blame to the manufacturer where appropriate.

Section 151C will pick up where the amended section 133A left off after a defendant deploys the "driverless vehicle defence." The statutory declaration will establish that the vehicle was a "driverless vehicle" at the time it was being parked and that therefore a "driverless vehicle parking offence" has been committed. This allows the enforcement agency to bring proceedings for a driverless vehicle offence under section 151C(1) and provides the evidence necessary to proceed against the manufacturer under paragraph (a) and subsection (6). The manufacturer then has the opportunity to provide evidence to displace this statutory declaration and undermine both the case against the manufacturer and the initial defendant's defence. If the manufacturer shows that the vehicle was not in a driverless mode at all, then section 151C will cease to apply, and proceedings will recommence against the initial defendant under section 133A. If the manufacturer shows that it was in a driverless mode but that it was not being used as directed, the proceedings will continue under section 151C but against the owner or possessor under subsection (1)(b) or (1)(c).

G. Vehicles in Ride-Sharing Fleets

In all of the preceding discussion, it has been assumed that when a person (or company) is using a driverless vehicle in a fully autonomous mode, then—as long as it is being used as directed—the manufacturer can be held liable for offences committed by the vehicle, such as speeding. This is because the manufacturer has represented that the vehicle is capable of handling itself, and so everything is dependent on the vehicle being able to live up to this representation. But as discussed earlier in this chapter, when the person or company using the driverless vehicle is deploying it as part of a ride-sharing fleet, there may be advantages in relying instead on their fleet management practices. So the fleet manager would be responsible for ensuring that that the vehicles were not directed to do anything outside of their capabilities. For example, if a customer requested a ride that would require the vehicle to operate in weather conditions or geographical areas or road conditions or configurations that the vehicle was not able to handle, then the fleet manager would have systems to ensure that a driverless vehicle was not allocated to that ride (and perhaps send out a human-driven vehicle or advise the customer that a suitable vehicle was not available). And if the guarantor of safety and legal compliance is these fleet management practices, then it makes more sense to hold the fleet manager liable if any offences were to result.

It is not necessary to have any additional provisions to allow this to happen. The manufacturer will be incentivised to make clear representations to the fleet manager as to the capabilities of their vehicles and to seek a contractual indemnification from the fleet manufacturer. So if a driverless vehicle in the fleet committed an offence, the fleet manager would be liable as the owner or possessor of the vehicle and would not be able to pass that liability to the manufacturer. A fleet manager would likely not even try to do this because it would be in breach of its contractual arrangement with the manufacturer. And to try and do so would either (i) not be possible under the provisions because the manufacturer would be able to show the vehicle was directed to operate outside of its operational design domain or (ii) be futile because the fleet manager would become liable for the cost of any fine anyway through the contractual indemnity.

Similar contractual arrangements could also be used for the customers of the ride-sharing fleet and for the owners of vehicles who lend their vehicles temporarily to the fleet. The important thing to note is that there need not be any specific statutory provision to facilitate these arrangements.

H. Use of Teleoperation

As discussed in chapter 3, it is possible that driverless vehicles may incorporate the capability for a remote human operator to take over control of the vehicle on occasion.

For example, a vehicle may find itself in a static situation that it cannot find a way out of. It may be stuck behind a vehicle that is inexplicably stopped and blocking the way. The vehicle may issue a call to a "support centre" where human operators are standing by to render assistance. If the vehicle was operating in a ride-sharing fleet, then the support centre might be provided by the fleet management company. Or the support centre might be provided by the manufacturer itself. The remote human operator can see what the vehicle "sees" through its cameras and will guide the vehicle slowly out of its predicament and back into circumstances where the vehicle can assume control again.

The chances of an offence being committed during such a low-speed manoeuvre seem small. But if it did happen, then the proposed provisions outlined previously should deal with it adequately. To all outside observers, the vehicle would appear to be operating in an autonomous mode with no human input. If the support centre was operated by the manufacturer, then the liability for the offence would wind its way through all the various provisions before ending up with the manufacturer. It would then, in theory, be possible for the manufacturer to provide evidence that the vehicle was actually being driven by a human (its employee) and redirect proceedings toward that individual. This might present difficulties for the enforcement agency, particularly if the individual was working in an offshore support centre. More likely, the manufacturer would treat the offence as having been committed by the vehicle and accept responsibility itself.

The situation would be the same if the support centre was operated by the fleet manager, except that the fleet manager would likely be the party that ended up accepting liability.

I. Manufacturers without a Legal Presence in New Zealand

A major potential difficulty with the system recommended here may be that some manufacturers might not have a legal presence in New Zealand. There is generally no ability to enforce a New Zealand fine in foreign jurisdictions. For this system to work, therefore, it may be necessary to insert a requirement in the Land Transport Act for manufacturers to have a legal presence in New Zealand in the form of a company with sufficient capitalisation or insurance to cover any fines that may result if their vehicles were to incur criminal liability. This requirement would be a condition before a vehicle could be certified for entry on New Zealand roads. It would also apply each time the vehicle was due for a new warrant.

It may also be necessary to make an amendment to the guarantees in sections 5 - 10 of the Consumer Guarantees Act 1993. This would set out that if a vehicle is not able to obtain a warrant of fitness due to the manufacturer failing to maintain a legal presence in New Zealand, then that vehicle would not be "of acceptable quality." This would then give the owner of the vehicle a right of redress under section 25 of the Consumer Guarantees Act 1993.

J. Software Updates

As discussed in chapter 6, complications can arise when software updates are not accepted by the consumer. My view is that this should be treated in much the same way as outlined in chapter 6. Ideally, the manufacturer will either (i) ensure updates happen automatically, (ii) not allow the vehicle to operate in driverless mode unless the updates are accepted, or (iii) warn an operator who tries to operate a driverless mode without the updates that the vehicle is now operating outside of its operational design domain and so the operator will be liable if anything goes wrong. If the manufacturer does none of these things, then the manufacturer would be liable for any offences.

K. Strict Compliance Versus Pragmatism

A common concern about driverless vehicles is that they will not be able to operate effectively if compelled to strictly comply with the law. This concern is based on the idea that there are situations where the drivers of vehicles must be pragmatic and commit minor breaches of the road rules. Examples of the situations that people are concerned about include the following:

- A vehicle encounters an obstruction—such as a parked vehicle—in the left-hand lane. If it is to proceed, it must illegally utilise the right-hand lane to drive around the obstruction.
- In certain crowded areas, pedestrians will routinely cross the road illegally in front of turning traffic that has the right of way, and vehicles will find it impossible to proceed unless they gently "nudge" their way through. This is illegal because vehicles are—for safety reasons—required to stop for pedestrians even when they are in the wrong.
- Motorists routinely drive above the speed limit on some sections of road, and driving at the speed limit is unsafe and provokes dangerous passing manoeuvres by other drivers.
- It is often necessary to exceed the limit in order to safely execute a passing manoeuvre. This situation may arise if a vehicle in front is driving just below the speed limit so that a vehicle that wants to drive at the speed limit must exceed it in order to complete the overtaking manoeuvre in the space available.

The concern is that requiring driverless vehicles to strictly comply with the law in these situations might prevent them from functioning safely and effectively. But closer examination of these supposedly problematic scenarios often reveals that this concern is unfounded.

Take the example about vehicles having to use the right lane to get around an obstruction. The relevant requirement here is clause 2.1(1) of the Land Transport (Road User) Rule 2004.

2.1 Keeping left

(1) A driver, when driving, must at all times drive as near as practicable to the left side of the roadway unless this rule otherwise provides.

This requirement has a practicability exemption built it into it, which could be used to justify using the right lane to drive around an obstacle. Such a driver is driving as near to the left as practicable, but it was necessary to dip into the right lane to get around the obstacle. If there was any doubt about this, it is removed by subclause (3) of clause 2.1, which allows a driver to drive in the right lane if the left lane is obstructed.

(3) A driver may drive in the right lane in the direction of travel when driving on a multi-lane road if—

    (a) the driver is turning right, or making a U-turn from the centre of the road, and is giving the prescribed signal of that driver's intention to turn right; or

    (b) the driver is passing; or

    (c) the left lane is unavailable to the driver; or

    (d) the driver is required by any provision of this rule to drive in the right lane; or

    (e) a variable lane control downward-facing arrow sign indicates that the driver must drive in the right lane; or

    (f) the driver is avoiding an obstruction; or

    (g) the traffic in all other lanes is congested; or

    (h) the traffic in every lane is congested.

The example about a vehicle having to "nudge" through pedestrians is similar. There is no obligation to give way to pedestrians unless they have the right of way. Obviously, it would be criminal to recklessly plough through such pedestrians, but there is nothing illegal about the necessary tactic of cautiously proceeding, provided the vehicle is not reckless and makes no contact with pedestrians.

For the other two examples (in which it is clear that the law is being broken), it is debatable as to whether selective noncompliance really is necessary or justifiable. If traffic is routinely speeding in a certain area, then either (i) the speed limit is too low and it needs to be raised or (ii) motorists are driving too fast and the introduction of driverless vehicles that actually obey the limit might be a welcome civilising influence. Similarly, is it really a problem if a following vehicle sometimes has to drive at ninety kilometres per hour for a while until a longer passing space opens up? If it is thought that vehicles should be able to speed while passing (and that this is worth the additional fatalities that would likely result), then the law could be changed to allow this.

If there really are situations where noncompliance with the law is necessary and desirable, then this is an existing problem with the law being insufficiently flexible. And the solution is that it needs to be amended for driverless and human-driven vehicles alike.

In the meantime, if social norms have evolved to compensate for supposed deficiencies in the law and allow for minor but necessary breaches, and if enforcement officers are exercising their discretion to recognise these norms, then driverless vehicles can be programmed to comply with these norms. There is no reason why officers shouldn't exercise this discretion consistently for driverless vehicles. If they did not, defendants would have excellent prospects to overturn any decision to take enforcement action against a driverless vehicle that was simply following accepted social norms that are tolerated or encouraged for human drivers.

L. Corporate Manslaughter

Earlier in this chapter there was discussion about how it makes no sense to impose a retributive penalty on the manufacturer of a vehicle that commits an offence, provided that the manufacturer was acting in good faith and legitimately attempting to develop a safe vehicle. As a result, the penalties proposed in this chapter are not retributive. They are not even really consequentialist—they are mainly just for the purpose of ensuring that driverless vehicles have to play by the same rules as other vehicles.

It would be a different story however if a manufacturer perpetrated some sort of major corporate malfeasance whereby it deliberately misrepresented the capability of a vehicle, and this led to deaths. If an individual did this then it could amount to manslaughter. The offence of manslaughter is defined in section 171 of the Crimes Act 1961 as "culpable homicide not amounting to murder". Under section 160(2) of the Crimes Act, homicide is culpable when it consists in the killing of any person "by an omission without lawful excuse to perform any legal duty". If a person has developed and released a driverless vehicle, then they are likely to have a duty under section 156 of the Crimes Act as a person who "makes …anything whatever, which in the absence of precaution or care, may endanger human life." That duty is to "take reasonable precautions against and to use reasonable care to avoid such danger" and a person is "criminally responsible for the consequences of omitting without lawful excuse to discharge that duty." If a person manufacturers a vehicle that has some limited driverless capability but fails to take the reasonable precaution of warning users of its severe limitations and misrepresents its capabilities, and this results in a death, then that person could be held to have breached the duty in section 156 and have committed the offence of manslaughter.

But manufacturers will invariably be corporate entities, which means two things. Firstly, responsibility will likely be too diffuse to show that any one individual within the company has breached the duty. Secondly, companies cannot be liable for the offence of manslaughter.

One would hope that the lack of a corporate manslaughter offence in New Zealand is not likely to be a problem because the manufacturers of driverless vehicles are unlikely to behave so badly that such an offence would be needed. If it is thought to be a problem then it is a wider issue than just driverless vehicles. The New Zealand Government is said to be currently looking at introducing a corporate manslaughter offence after the inability of police to prosecute anyone for the collapse of the CTV Building in the 2011 Christchurch earthquake.[157]

Recommendations

Make the amendments and insertions to the Land Transport Act 1998 as suggested in the text to create two new offences: (i) a driverless vehicle

---

157 Matthew Theunissen. "Govt Considering Introducing Corporate Manslaughter Law to enable CTV Prosecution". New Zealand Herald. 1 December 2017.

offence and (ii) a driverless vehicle parking offence. The question of who is liable for these offences and when is determined by whether the vehicle was driving itself using an unsupervised autonomous mode of operation within the operational design domain of that mode.

9

Regulation of Testing

Many jurisdictions around the world have legal requirements that have to be met by companies that are testing driverless vehicles on public roads.

For example, the State of California has had regulations in place since 2014 governing the testing of driverless vehicles on Californian roads.[158] These regulations require companies to obtain permits to test. These companies are then required to provide the California Department of Motor Vehicles (DMV) with a report for every traffic accident involving a driverless vehicle within ten business days of the accident. They are also required to submit an annual report summarizing the "disengagements" of driverless technology during testing. These disengagements relate to vehicles that are being tested with a safety driver sitting in the driver's seat with a steering wheel and all the usual controls. A disengagement is essentially an event where the vehicle "decides" that it needs to hand over control of the vehicle to the safety driver. As of 30 November 2017, the California DMV had issued forty-two driverless vehicle testing permits. These included well-known companies, such as Volkswagen, Mercedes-Benz, Waymo, Tesla, Nissan, GM, BMW, Honda, Ford, Baidu, Subaru, Nvidia, Navya, Apple, Samsung, Uber, and Lyft, plus a host of less well-known companies. It had received fifty-one accident reports from companies, such as GM, Waymo, Uber, and Nissan. Most of these were

---

158 https://www.dmv.ca.gov/portal/dmv/detail/vr/autonomous+/testing.

very minor accidents, and none of them were serious. The disengagement reports from the various companies revealed widely varying numbers of disengagements between the companies, but it was hard to draw any conclusions from these reports because of the different ways that companies were testing their vehicles. There was also some uncertainty about what counted as testing. For example, Tesla utilises data collected when its customers are using the vehicle's autopilot mode. These could be viewed as being akin to tests of a driverless vehicle system with a safety driver. But they are not classified as such, so there are no reports made about accidents of disengagements. In 2016, Uber had a high-profile dispute with the California DMV about whether its use of driverless vehicles with a safety driver to pick up Uber customers qualified as tests for which it needed a permit.[159] Uber thought they did not. The DMV disagreed, and in December 2016, it revoked the registrations of the sixteen driverless vehicles that Uber was using for its California programme. Uber eventually applied for and obtained the permit in March 2017.

New Zealand does not presently have any regulation of driverless vehicle testing. Instead, the NZTA has a policy to encourage companies to submit a safety management plan for approval.[160]

In my view, there is no need to change this. The essential point is that driving a vehicle on a public road in New Zealand for the purposes of a test is not treated any differently by the law than driving a vehicle for any other purpose. If a vehicle is not competent to drive without a supervising driver, then it should not be driving on a public road without a supervising driver, regardless of whether it is for test or not. Chapter 5 outlines how existing laws can be utilised to prevent the use of vehicles without a driver when this is unsafe. This would apply to any vehicle on a public road, whether it was being used for a test or not.

---

159 Darryl Etherington, "Uber Gets Its Self-Driving Vehicle Test Permit in California," *TechCrunch*, 9 March 2017.

160 https://www.nzta.govt.nz/vehicles/vehicle-types/automated-and-autonomous -vehicles/testing-autonomous-vehicles-in-new-zealand/.

The acquisition of disengagement and accident reports is not that useful, and the imposition of these regulatory burdens on companies might discourage testing in New Zealand. The State of California might be able to get away with imposing such requirements on companies without unduly discouraging testing and investment, but New Zealand, given its size and distance, probably wouldn't.

10

> The most disturbing manoeuvre came when they cut the Jeep's brakes, leaving me frantically pumping the pedal as the two-ton SUV slid uncontrollably into a ditch.
>
> —ANDY GREENBERG

In July 2015, *Wired* magazine published an account by a writer who had volunteered to participate in a vehicle hacking demonstration.[161] As he drove a 2014 Jeep Cherokee down the highway in St. Louis, a pair of professional hackers named Charlie Miller and Chris Valasek blasted him with music, turned on the air conditioning, squirted wiper fluid, activated the wipers, and—most worrying of all on a busy highway with fast-moving traffic—cut the transmission and slowed the vehicle to a crawl. Later, when the vehicle was in the safer environs of a carpark, they disabled the brakes and allowed the vehicle to slowly roll forward into a ditch. All of this was done remotely over the Internet by the hackers sitting in their house miles away to a vehicle that had not been altered in any way and had no devices attached to it.

---

161 Andy Greenberg, "Hackers Remotely Kill a Jeep on the Highway—with Me in It," *Wired*, 7 November 2015.

This was all possible because many modern vehicles now have Internet connected features for entertainment and navigation. The hackers shared their research with Chrysler, the manufacturer of the vehicle, which released a patch to secure vehicles against the vulnerability (which ironically could not itself be deployed remotely; it needed to be implemented manually via a USB stick). There is nothing particularly special or vulnerable about Chrysler vehicles. The hackers had to concentrate their resources on a particular model but could have picked others. Since their 2015 demonstration, Miller and Valasek have perfected even more alarming hacks, including the ability to steer the vehicle into oncoming traffic at speed.

Vehicle cybersecurity is an issue for driverless vehicles, but this example—which involved a "regular" vehicle with no driverless capability—shows that the concern is not unique to driverless vehicles. It is an issue for all modern vehicles with an Internet connection. Jurisdictions around the world are currently grappling with the best way to address this new risk. Vehicle standards relied upon all over the world to ensure the safety of vehicles do not currently have any prescriptive requirements for vehicle cybersecurity. All that currently exists are guidelines, such as that released by the US National Highway Traffic Safety Administration (NHTSA) in October 2016.[162] It may be that vehicle standards will eventually incorporate such requirements.

In the meantime, it is important to have some mechanisms to try to ensure the safety of driverless vehicles against cybersecurity threats. In chapter 5, this report recommends that New Zealand should do this by utilising voluntary safety self-assessments modelled on those that NHTSA's latest automated vehicles policy[163] encourages manufacturers to produce. This policy already contains a section on vehicle cybersecurity, which encourages manufacturers to document how cybersecurity is addressed;

---

162 National Highway Traffic Safety Administration. *Cybersecurity Best Practices for Modern Vehicles* (Report No. DOT HS 812 333) (Washington, DC: Author, 2016).
163 Automated Driving Systems 2.0: A Vision for Safety (September 2017).

report incidents, threats, and vulnerabilities; and share information across the industry to facilitate collaborative learning. As with any aspect of a vehicle driverless system, manufacturers could face regulatory action in the United States if NHTSA does not consider cybersecurity has been adequately addressed.

Reliance on safety assessments that take cybersecurity into account is probably the best that New Zealand can do unless and until overseas standards are developed, and this report does not recommend any further action at the present moment.

Mandated Vehicle Connectivity and Radio Spectrum Use

One of the hopes for driverless vehicles, as outlined in chapter 1, is that they will be able to be effectively network and allow traffic to be rationally coordinated. Vehicles would no longer need to wait at intersections because the perpendicular traffic stream would "know" when a vehicle is coming and adjust to create a gap. Long columns of traffic could speed up and slow down as a single unit. This has huge potential to reduce congestion and emissions and improve energy efficiency.

But of course such coordination will not be possible unless and until there are at least some roads or lanes that are reserved for driverless vehicles. Having a single human-driven vehicle in the mix would foul everything up. It also will not be possible unless and until all the driverless vehicles are communicating with each other and with coordination infrastructure. The question then arises as to whether any regulation is required to allow this to happen. Should there be a legal requirement for all vehicles to have the capacity to communicate with other vehicles and infrastructure? And should there be a portion of the electromagnetic spectrum reserved for communication to and from vehicles?

The potential for vehicle-to-vehicle (known as "V2V") and vehicle-to-infrastructure (known as "V2X") communication to improve the safety and efficiency of transportation has a relatively long history that predates the more recent artificial-intelligence-based advances in transport. It falls within a wider category of technologies known as Intelligent Transport

Systems ("ITS"). The US federal initiatives from the 1990s to build the first fully automated roadway (as described in chapter 2) that culminated in 1997's Automated Free Agent Demonstration relied in part on V2V and V2X communication. Since 2000, the United States has reserved the frequency range of 5850 to 5925 MHz for V2V and V2X communication. Other jurisdictions have also allocated spectrum for ITS applications but not the exact same parts of the spectrum. Europe reserves the smaller upper portion of the US allocation (5875 to 5925MHz). Japan has allocated 5770 to 5850 MHz for ITS, though this must also be used for electronic tolling. Due to spectrum congestion, Japan has also allocated 755.5 to 764.5 MHz for ITS (which may cause problems when Japanese vehicles are imported into New Zealand, due to the fact that possession of transmitting devices that use this frequency in New Zealand is illegal without a licence). In both Australia and New Zealand frequencies in the 5900 MHz band are reserved for ITS purposes, though are currently unused.

The United States has also had plans to legislate to require vehicle manufacturers to include radios in their vehicles that would allow for vehicles to use ITS technologies in the reserved part of the spectrum. In December 2016, the US Department of Transportation released a proposed rule to do just this.[164] The hope was that this would eventually prevent many crashes by informing vehicles of impending danger and issuing warnings to drivers or even triggering automatic braking. It is not clear at present whether this proposed rule will become law. The commercial uptake and use of ITS technology has been very slow, and some of the previous enthusiasm for ITS has been waning with a growing perception among some that it is an older approach that is being overtaken by the advent of modern driverless vehicles utilising sensors and artificial

---

164 "US DOT Advances Deployment of Connected Vehicle Technology to Prevent Hundreds of Thousands of Crashes," US Department of Transportation Press Release, 13 December 2016, at https://www.nhtsa.gov/press-releases/us-dot-advances-deployment-connected-vehicle-technology-prevent-hundreds-thousands.

intelligence. The reality is more complicated, in that modern driverless vehicles have made V2V and V2X communication both less important (in the short term) and more important (in the medium to long term).

In the short term, it is less important because driverless vehicles can drive themselves and avoid crashes without the need for such wireless communication. They can get all the information they need from their sensors, GPS, and preloaded 3-D maps. As noted in chapter 2, this is the crucial factor driving the optimistic forecasts for driverless vehicle adoption. The utility of ITS technologies was greatly dependent on infrastructure and on other vehicles also having ITS capability. But the new driverless vehicles can function and be useful even if there is no additional infrastructure and no other driverless vehicles on the road.

In the medium to long term, V2V and V2X communication has tremendous potential to amplify the benefits of driverless vehicles. A driverless vehicle controlled by a computer will be able to put the information it receives from other vehicles and infrastructure to much more effective use than would a human driver or a "dumb" automatic braking system. This is where we could see the realisation of the dream of citywide coordination of traffic to speedily whisk people and goods to their destinations without traffic jams.

An important consideration to note for the future is the risk that this dream of traffic jams being choreographed into nonexistence also has the potential to become an Orwellian nightmare. Ideally the coordination mechanism would happen in much the same way that information moving around the Internet is coordinated, with no overall centralised authority. But a decentralised system is much more vulnerable to cyberattack and—while society might tolerate this with respect to the Internet—it is a different story when a whole city of moving vehicles is hacked. A centralised system under government control would be more resilient to attack but brings huge concerns about the potential for government surveillance and control of individuals. This prospect was recently identified as being ethically questionable in the German Ethics Code for Automated and

Connected Driving.[165] Fortunately, this is not a decision that needs to be confronted yet, and there is hope that a technological solution will mean that cities and their citizens will not have to choose between freedom of mobility and freedom from oppressive surveillance and control.

The same is true with respect to the wider question of mandated connectivity. Because there are no short-term advantages of this connectivity, my view is that it is not yet necessary for New Zealand to make decisions about mandating connectivity. Mandated connectivity might be valuable in countries like the United States that manufacture a lot of vehicles, because it can act as a stimulus to accelerate and standardise the uptake of the technology. This does not apply in a country like New Zealand without major vehicle manufacturing. It would be better to be "technology agnostic" for now. For all we know, it could become unnecessary to reserve part of the spectrum for vehicle use or to use dedicated in-built transmitters. It is not currently practicable for vehicles to use the cellular network like any other devices (a little bit of latency can be tolerated for your iPad but not your vehicle). But this might change.

---

165 See discussion of Ethical Guideline 13 in Christoph Luetge, "The German Ethics Code for Automated and Connected Driving," *Philos. Technol.* 30 (2017): 547–558. Guideline 13 states that "The complete connectivity and central control of all motor vehicles within the context of a digital transport infrastructure is ethically questionable if, and to the extent that, it is unable to safely rule out the total surveillance of road users and manipulation of vehicle control."

12

Urban Planning

One of the great concerns about driverless vehicles is that they could transform cities for the worse. Many cities rely on foot traffic for their unique character. If everyone has super-cheap point-to-point transport on demand, might our cities degenerate into featureless urban deserts populated by hyper efficient people-moving boxes?

Some of the potential solutions to these kinds of problems lie with city planners. But if planners are instructed to find solutions, do they have the legal powers to put them into practice?

One possible solution is to close off parts of the city to vehicles so that people are dropped off at central points and must walk the "last mile." There would need to be exceptions, such as for loading vehicles or for people with disabilities.

There are existing legislative provisions that could be used to achieve this. Under section 342 of the Local Government Act 1974, a council has the power to "stop" a road (that is, extinguish its legal character as a road). The council must go through a notification and consultation process, and may declare the road stopped if no objections are received. If objections are received, the council must refer the proposal to stop the road to the Environment Court to decide.

Given that it is likely that the council would still want to allow vehicles through the stopped road for some purposes, a better solution might be to declare the targeted roads to be "pedestrian malls." Under section 336 of the Local Government Act 1974, a council may declare a road or part of a road to be a pedestrian mall for which the driving of vehicles is prohibited. The declaration can include the kinds of exemptions that would be needed for disabled people or others with a need to drive a vehicle all the way to their destination. The Act provides for suitable controls on a council's use of this power by requiring a special consultative procedure that provides an opportunity for people to present their views and appeal to the Environment Court if they do not like the decision.

The same mechanisms would be available in suburban areas, where they may be demanded by local residents to convert roads to common outdoor living space, particularly in the case of cul-de-sacs. If all the residents in a small cul-de-sac no longer own cars and use ride-sharing services, then they may wish to close the street off from vehicles for most purposes.

Another concern is that driverless vehicles, for all their anticipated congestion- and emission-easing potential, might actually increase traffic. If they are really going to be as cheap and convenient as hoped, then we might expect to see the average person taking a lot more vehicle trips.

One of the ways this could be addressed could be through congestion charges in high-traffic-density areas. Congestion charging schemes have already been implemented in a number of overseas cities, such as Singapore (1975), London (2003), and Stockholm (2007). Revenue from the scheme can be put into improving public transport (as is the case in London) in order to provide people with an incentive, as well as a disincentive, to limit the use of private vehicles. These schemes have had some success in reducing congestion. The Singapore scheme was dramatically effective when it was first introduced in 1975, reducing vehicle numbers by 76 percent.[166] The results in London and Stockholm were also significant but much more modest. London saw a 16 percent reduction in

---

166 A. Spencer and C. Sien, "National Policy Towards Cars: Singapore," *Transport Reviews* 5 no. 4 (1985), 301–324.

vehicle numbers after three years.[167] Stockholm saw an immediate reduction and persistent reduction of 22 percent.[168]

With the advent of driverless vehicles, there would be opportunities to tweak these schemes to try to improve their effectiveness.

There are no existing legislative mechanisms in New Zealand that could be used to set up a congestion charging scheme in any of our cities. While there is a mechanism in the Land Transport Management Act 2003 that allows for road-tolling schemes to be set up,[169] the purpose of these schemes needs to be the provision of funds for the construction of roads. The use of such a scheme to disincentivise vehicle use would likely be regarded as ultra vires. Hence, it would be necessary to enact some empowering legislation, similar to the UK legislation that allowed for the London congestion charge.[170]

---

167 *Impacts Monitoring*—Fifth Annual Report, Transport for London, June 2007.

168 J. Eliasson, "The Stockholm Congestion Charges: An Overview," CTS Working Paper, 2014, 7.

169 Section 46 of the Land Transport Management Act 2003 allows for the establishment of a road tolling scheme by Order-in-Council. This has been used to set up toll roads, such as Northern Gateway Toll Road (see Land Transport Management (Road Tolling Scheme for Northern Gateway) Order 2005).

170 The Greater London Authority Act 1999 included provision for road-user charging schemes (schedule 23) and workplace charging levies (schedule 24).

Use of Special Lanes

As discussed in chapter 3, there may be advantages in providing dedicated and separated lanes for use by autonomous shuttles or buses. This would allow for a zone that is physically closed off from potential hazards. Whether there is a need for such closed-off lanes may be somewhat debatable however. If driverless vehicles improve as quickly as is hoped, then the benefit of having closed-off lanes may be a short-term phenomenon, and public authorities might come to regret spending the large sums required to constrict them.

But there is a more compelling reason for having dedicated lanes for autonomous vehicles. As discussed in chapter 11, there is huge potential for driverless traffic to be networked in order to reduce congestion. This potential can only be fully realised if there are at least some roads or lanes that are reserved for the exclusive use of driverless vehicles. This could perhaps begin with a driverless vehicle lane on the motorway, which would allow whole columns of traffic to speed up and slow down as a single unit. The question then arises as to whether law reform is needed to allow such lanes to be created, if it is decided that they are desirable.

The answer seems to be that no such reform is necessary. Under section 22AB(1)(r) of the Land Transport Act 1998, road-controlling authorities are able to make bylaws prescribing "that on any road any traffic lane may be used…only by vehicles of specified classes or vehicles carrying specified classes of loads or no fewer than a specified number of occupants." This bylaw has been used to create lanes that cannot be used by single-occupant cars (in order to reduce congestion by encouraging car-pooling) or that can only be used by buses. An example of this is the northern busway on the North Shore of Auckland. The New Zealand Land Transport Agency created this busway[171] using the power in section 22AB. It restricts use of the busway to heavy buses and airport shuttles that have applied to use it and been approved. There does not appear to be any reason why section 22AB could not be used to prescribe lanes for the use of driverless vehicles.

---

171 See Bylaw 2008/01, Prescribing Use of the Northern Busway in Auckland.

Driverless vehicles will collect a lot of data. They will keep records of where they have been and when. When they serve in driverless fleets, they will know who is riding in them and when they got in and got out. And as they travel around multiple onboard video cameras and other sensors will record their surroundings. Much of this information is likely to be uploaded to servers operated by the manufacturer and other companies.

This obviously has significant implications for privacy. All of this information could be utilised to build profiles of individuals and then used in dubious ways by insurance companies, employers, or governments.

This is an issue that is not unique to driverless vehicles. Many non-driverless vehicles already collect and store locational and video data. And mobile phones have been keeping a record of your travels for years. You may not remember where you went on this day three years ago, but the companies that provide locational services on your phone probably do.

New Zealand already has legislation that is designed to protect individuals against misuse of their personal data. It applies to "agencies" which is essentially everyone (individuals and public and private bodies) who collects and holds personal information, with a few exceptions (such as the news media). It sets out twelve information privacy principles that regulate how personal information may be collected, held, used, and disclosed. For example, agencies must disclose when they collect personal information, keep information secure and must not use it for a different purpose than that for which it was collected or disclose it to others (unless certain exemptions apply).

If an agency breaches these principles, then the affected person may complain to the Privacy Commissioner, who will try to facilitate a settlement between the parties. If this fails, then the matter can go to the Human Rights Review Tribunal, which can require remedial action and award damages of up to $200,000.

In 2011, the New Zealand Law Commission carried out a review of the Privacy Act[172] and specifically examined the issue of whether it was up to the task of safeguarding privacy against the barrage of new challenges presented by new technology. It concluded that the Act did provide sufficient protection for now but noted that this needed to be kept under regular review as technology continued to develop.[173]

Driverless vehicles are a significant new technological development, but, in my view, they do not present any new privacy issues that were not around and considered by the Law Commission when it reached its conclusions in 2011. I believe the Law Commission's conclusions are still accurate, and they apply to driverless vehicles. No amendments to privacy law are required as a result of driverless vehicles, and any future amendments should be developed by considering the overall effects of new technology, not just driverless vehicles.

---

172 Law Commission of New Zealand, Review of the Privacy Act 1993: Review of the Law of Privacy Stage 4, June 2011, Wellington, New Zealand, Report 123.
173 See para 10.6 of the report.

Standards for Parking

As discussed in earlier chapters, the parking habits of driverless vehicles will be potentially very different. When your vehicle drops you off and drives away, there is no need to have car parking available close to a destination.

Driverless vehicles that are providing transport as part of a driverless fleet will likely spend a lot less of their time parked, as they will be heading off to serve more customers. When driverless vehicles do need to park, they might be better served by parking buildings on the city fringe, where real estate is less expensive. And if more and more people are preferring to use cheap mobility services provided by driverless vehicle fleets rather than incur the expense of owning a vehicle, then there is less need for private residences to have car parks.

All of this means that it will probably be necessary to revise some of the requirements that relate to parking in New Zealand cities.

At a national level, the New Zealand Building Code requires that parking spaces within a building "shall be constructed to permit safe and easy unloading and movement of vehicles, and to avoid conflict between vehicles and pedestrians."[174] This would create needless inefficiencies for new parking buildings built specifically to cater for driverless vehicles. The vehicles would enter such buildings without any passengers on board, so

---

174 See D1.2.2 of the New Zealand Building Code. The Building Code is contained in regulations made under the Building Act 2004.

there would not need to be as much space to allow for easy unloading and no need to avoid conflict with pedestrians.

At a local level, many district plans have rules that require new building developments to provide for new parking to cater for the additional demand that the development is expected to generate. For example, the Wellington City District Plan requires the creation of visitor parking for multiunit developments in residential areas.[175] The need for the plan to impose these requirements on developers should be re-evaluated.

The Wellington City District Plan also requires[176] parking to be provided and maintained in accordance with sections 1, 2, and 5 of the joint Australian and New Zealand Standard 2890.1 2004, Parking Facilities, Part 1: Off Street Car Parking.[177] This sets out minimum widths for car parks, and these widths are unnecessarily wide for driverless cars that do not require space for people to open doors and get out.

Recommendation 7

Amend the New Zealand Building Code to remove requirements for parking spaces that are unnecessarily restrictive for driverless vehicles.

Recommendation 8

Territorial authorities should re-evaluate requirements for developers to provide parking in the vicinity of the development, in order to recognise the likelihood that driverless vehicles can drive away and park elsewhere (if they need to park).

---

175 See rule 5.6.1.3 of the Wellington City District Plan, which requires a minimum of one dedicated space for every four household units for any proposal that results in seven units or more.

176 See for examples rule 5.6.1.3 and rule 13.6.1.3.2.

177 See section 2.4.1(b) joint Australian and New Zealand Standard 2890.1 2004.

16

Even if driverless vehicles are as safe as is hoped, no technology is ever perfect. Some crashes will still be unavoidable. There is much speculation that driverless vehicles may soon be faced with decisions as to different courses of evasive action that will result in different levels and different kinds of harm. Should the vehicle carry on straight and kill the pedestrian or swerve into the wall and kill its passenger? This raises questions as to how vehicles should be programmed to choose. Should they always attempt to choose the option that results in the lowest net harm to human life? Is it ethical to program the vehicles to value some lives (e.g., the lives of its passengers) over others? What about the lives of animals or damage to property? Should the law prescribe how vehicles should be programmed?

Philosophers, journalists, ethicists, and other practitioners of the field of "trolleyology"[178] have been enthusiastically constructing elaborate thought experiments involving driverless vehicles to explore these ramifications.

---

178 The field of "trolleyology" dates back to 1967 following a paper by P. Foot (1967), "The Problem of Abortion and the Doctrine of the Double Effect in Virtues and Vices," *Oxford Review* 5 (1967): 5–15. It refers to a series of thought experiments involving variations on the trolley problem, in which a person has to decide whether to passively let a trolley continue on its course and collide with and kill five people or actively divert it and kill a single person. The insights gained from these thought experiments are often touted as being informative in analysing questions about driverless vehicle ethics.

A typical example, called the *tunnel case*, is set out by Jan Gogoll and Julian Müller in a recent article[179] on the topic.

> Imagine you are sitting in your autonomous car going at a steady pace entering a tunnel. In front of you is a school bus with children on board going at the same pace as you are. In the left lane there is a single car with two passengers overtaking you. For some reason the bus in front of you brakes and your car cannot brake to avoid crashing into the bus. There are three different strategies your car can follow: First, brake and crash into the bus, which will result in the loss of lives on the bus. Second, steer into the passing car on your left—pushing it into the wall, saving your life but killing the other car's two passengers. Third, it can steer itself (and you) into the right hand sidewall of the tunnel, sacrificing you but sparing all other participants' lives.

This article goes on to convincingly argue that there should be government regulation requiring manufacturers to program vehicles so that they would always choose minimum harm options, such as option three. It explains why this would produce a better result for everyone and how even people who want to selfishly maximise their own welfare should still agree with this approach. To do otherwise, they argue, would result in an undesirable manifestation of the prisoner's dilemma.

The prisoner's dilemma is a classic example of game theory in which two criminal associates ("A" and "B") are kept in separate cells and offered a deal by prosecutors to betray the other in exchange for a lesser charge. If both associates betray each other, they both get two years in prison. If one is loyal and is betrayed by the other, then the loyal associate gets three years in prison, and the traitor is rewarded with freedom. The optimum net result is if they both remain loyal, in which case, they both

179 Jan Gogoll and Julian Müller, "Autonomous Cars: In Favor of a Mandatory Ethics Setting," *Sci Eng Ethics* 23 (2017): 681–700.

179

get one year. But because of the risk of betrayal, the rational strategy for both is to betray the other. The prisoner's dilemma is related to the "tragedy of the commons" and is helpful in explaining and finding solutions for many societal problems, such as overfishing, doping in sports, and disarmament.

When applied to a city full of driverless cars, the concern is that every individual will "betray" their fellow citizens by selecting a vehicle that prioritises their personal survival and that this will lead to a suboptimal outcome. All members of society could at some stage in their life be (or be related to) a person who is at the receiving end of a "selfish" decision by a driverless vehicle. This means that the best way of maximising the chances of survival for themselves or their loved ones is for the government to legally require manufacturers to program vehicles to choose the option that results in the lowest loss of life.[180]

It's a clever argument. But it glosses over some details that could—if taken into account—result in quite a different calculus.

The first and most obvious issue is that the tunnel case is extremely contrived and not very believable. We are told that option 1 (crashing into the bus) will result in the deaths of multiple children riding on it. How can this be so certain? And the scenario seems to get this the wrong way around; a smaller vehicle rear-ending a large bus seems more likely to result in injuries and death for the person in the smaller vehicle. Perhaps this is just an artefact of a poorly designed scenario and can be easily addressed. To some extent, this is true. We could change the scenario so that the children are riding in a small car followed by a huge driverless SUV. Or perhaps we could say that the back of the bus has popped open, and children are spilling out onto the road. By tweaking the scenario like this, you might end up with something where the casualty rates of the

---

180 Calculating which option results in the lowest loss of life would of course be extremely complicated. As one wag pointed out, a car programmed to minimise loss of human life should drive its owner to Oxfam and suggest a sizable donation.

different options are more certain and believable, and the vehicle really does have genuine quandary to decide.

This brings us to the next issue, which is that the tunnel case is hopelessly inconsistent in its assumptions about the abilities of driverless vehicles. On the one hand, it overestimates these abilities by assuming that the vehicle knows all sorts of things that it could not possibly know, at least not now and not for the first few generations of driverless vehicles. How can it know that there are multiple children on the bus? How does it know, for that matter, that there is *anyone* on the bus other than the driver? How does it know how many people are in the other car? It may not even know how many passengers it is carrying itself. And even if it did know these things, how is it able to calculate such precise estimates as to how many people would die in the different scenarios? This will depend on many factors that the vehicle would not know. Are passengers wearing seatbelts? Are there airbags? What is the safety rating of the other vehicles? Are they well maintained with good tires and brakes? How will the other individuals or vehicles react?

At the same time, it is underestimating the ability of the vehicle to avoid the accident. We are told that the bus stops suddenly for some reason and the following driverless vehicle is unable to stop or even slow down enough to avoid an impact of epic and ultimately fatal proportions. But why is the scenario assuming that the driverless vehicle cannot stop in time? The great advantage of driverless vehicles is that they can be programmed to avoid getting into these horrendous quandaries in the first place. Driverless vehicles can be programmed to maintain a following distance and velocity that is sufficient to stop in time, however suddenly the bus may stop. If the driverless vehicle cannot stop in time in the tunnel case, then there must surely be some other factor (oil on the road?) that is responsible. In which case, the driverless vehicle may be exhibiting a technical deficiency (if you think it is reasonable to expect driverless cars to detect oil on the road), but there is no ethical quandary. When a vehicle "thinks" it can stop in time, there is no quandary. The best decision it can make—based on the available information—is to brake without swerving in either direction.

And this is highly likely to be the case for most thought experiments we can dream up. Slamming on the brakes is going to be unambiguously the best choice the vast majority of the time. If the car can stop in time, then why swerve? It just introduces extra variables and danger. It is difficult to construct scenarios where any other course of action would be preferable from anybody's perspective. Someone might posit the case of a driverless car in a suburban environment that is faced with a child who has suddenly emerged onto the road from behind a bush. But if the vehicle is driving in an area that contains objects that can hide incoming pedestrians like this, then it should be programmed to assume—as a prudent human driver would—that this could happen. It should drive at an appropriate speed so it can stop if necessary.

It seems likely then that most manufacturers will not give their vehicles the capability to weigh up choices about whether to swerve or brake. They will program them to drive in such a way that braking alone will be sufficient as a universal strategy to minimise harm. Cases where swerving is better (for anyone) than braking will be so rare that it is probably not worth programming the car to do anything other than brake. And even if there are rare cases where it turns out that swerving would have been the better option, it is unlikely that the car would have enough information to reliably identify these cases and act accordingly.

It may be that in the future driverless vehicles will have access to the vastly larger quantities of information that would be necessary to produce the kind of omniscience that most thought experiments seem to presume they have (in order to estimate in such detail and precision the casualties associated with different options and to calculate that swerving is better than braking). But if driverless vehicles ever become *that* omniscient, then it is likely that their capabilities for avoiding getting into quandaries in the first place will be magnified to such an extent that it will still not be necessary to program vehicles to do anything other than brake.

In other words, a world with mandatory ethics prescribed by the government would likely be indistinguishable from a world where manufacturers were free to leave braking as the universal evasive strategy.

Maybe this will change in the future, but in my view, it would be unwise for New Zealand to act now and legislate for some sort of mandatory ethics setting for driverless vehicles. It is unlikely to do any good and may do significant harm if it is perceived as meaningless and cumbersome red tape and discourages manufacturers from introducing their vehicles in New Zealand. It might well go down in history as a well-meaning safety measure that actually cost lives, increased emissions and energy use, and sabotaged the country's future economic opportunities.